C000139560

BEAT DEPR

BEAT
DEPRESSION

Updated
and
EXTENDED
2022
Edition

DAVID M HINDS

BEAT DEPRESSION
Copyright © 2022 by David M Hinds

All rights reserved. This book or any portion thereof may not be reproduced or used
in any manner whatsoever without the express written permission of the publisher,
except for the use of brief quotations in a book review.

David M Hinds asserts the moral right to be identified as the author of this work.

The original version of this book was published by
Hodder and Stoughton (UK) in 2001
in the United States of America in 2002 by HarperCollins,

Arabic language edition published by
Jarir Bookstore in 2005.

A revised edition was published in 2019 by Luminaire Press, USA

Cover design by Claire Flint Last
Published by Blue Poppy Publishing Devon

ISBN: 978-1-83778-006-8

TO

ALL THE DEPRESSED PEOPLE
IN THE WORLD.

I have been where you are now and I admire you for reading your way out of depression. Work with me through the book and I promise you, you will be in a better place than you are now. Because of the nature of your condition, I've made it really easy to get started. Just one tick in the appropriate box is all I ask of you for now and then your journey of recovery is in motion.

IMPORTANT NOTE

This book is not intended to be a substitute for
medical advice or treatment. Any person with
a condition requiring medical attention should
consult a qualified medical practitioner.

Contents

PART ONE
Depressed

PART TWO
Why Me?

PART FIVE

Therapy

PART SIX

More Therapy

1

You are not alone

I HAVE BEEN WHERE YOU ARE NOW.
I WILL WRITE FOR YOU AND
YOU WILL READ FOR ME.

Today is the day we get started.

Depression, like the common cold, is an illness that can affect anyone, including the rich and famous. One in five of us will be affected by the condition at some stage in our lives. Like most other illnesses, when correctly diagnosed, it can be treated successfully. Depression, although frightening, is never permanent. It does not reduce our value as human beings. Are you depressed? If so, how depressed? Let's begin to find out.

In order to ascertain the best and safest way forward, you must decide how depressed you are on a scale of 0-5. Your choice should reflect how you have been feeling generally over the last two or three weeks. Don't worry if your selection is not quite right. Give yourself permission to adopt a trial and error approach. We can always put things right later when we under-stand more about your prevailing mood, your circumstances, your feelings, your psychological make-up and the overall structure of your thinking patterns. Please go ahead now and tick the box overleaf that seems most applicable to you

❑ 0) NOT DEPRESSED

❑ 1) MILDLY DEPRESSED

❑ 2) MODERATELY DEPRESSED

❑ 3) SEVERELY DEPRESSED

❑ 4) EXTREMES OF HIGHS AND LOWS

❑ 5) SUICIDAL

It may be that you will revise your choice later but this is a valuable starting point. If you have ticked (0) above, perhaps you are a loved one, family member, caring friend or professional acquaintance of someone whom you believe may be suffering from depression. If this is the case, it is probable you will read this book in a different way from a depressed person. You will be in a position to heighten your awareness and gain valuable insights into this much-misunderstood condition.

If you have ticked (1) to (5) let me begin by reassuring you. Due to a new generation of therapies and the widespread availability of non-addictive and highly effective drugs, the chances of recovering from depression quickly and safely have greatly increased. Your degree of depression will be dealt with in succeeding chapters.

Depression is best understood by observing its effects. The most obvious sign of depression is a persistent downturn in mood. Depression has a way of creeping up on you and dulling your feelings. You begin to lose interest in what is going on around you. You may feel sad, alone and isolated and cry for no apparent reason. You may assume a vacant, emotionless facial expression and you may feel guilty about things which happened in the past. Sometimes, with a different form of depression, feelings of sadness can alternate with sensations of elation or excitement but this may be a mask for unhappiness.

In everyday language, we have a tendency to speak of feeling depressed when our transitory downturn in mood simply relates to a routine or minor setback—perhaps the prospect of returning to work on Monday morning after a particularly enjoyable weekend. On the other hand, depression as an illness implies a severe emotional disturbance, the source of which may or may not be traceable to external causes.

We all feel down from time to time. Sadness is a normal part of life. Happiness would hold little meaning for us if we were untouched by sadness. But when sadness takes an almost permanent hold of us and seldom returns to joy, the likely cause is clinical depression, also known as major depression.

No one is immune from depression. It strikes people from all social groups, all countries and all cultural backgrounds. *A staggering 300 million people are affected in the world today!*

The death toll from depression is formidable: more people commit suicide every year than die in road accidents around the world. Statistically, at least 10 per cent of the clinically depressed (whether diagnosed as such or not) will take their own lives. The impact of that one, irreversible action on their families, friends and loved ones will be enormous.

Let's make further progress by examining where you are right now. It will be illuminating and helpful if you tick the boxes alongside any of the following statements that you believe are applicable to you. Once again, don't be afraid of making mistakes and bear in mind that your choice should once again reflect how you have been feeling over the last two or three weeks. It is a general picture of your state of mind that we are forming here, not a medical diagnosis.

Most of the time, do you*

- ❑ feel sad?
- ❑ feel helpless?
- ❑ feel tired?
- ❑ feel guilty about things?

- ❑ feel life is pointless?
- ❑ feel as if you are moving in slow motion?
- ❑ feel anxious or cry a lot?
- ❑ feel pessimistic or worthless?
- ❑ have difficulty concentrating?
- ❑ have difficulty making decisions?

Lately, have you*

- ❑ isolated yourself from others? Or wanted to?
- ❑ lost interest in things that used to give you pleasure?
- ❑ experienced problems at work, in school, at university or away from home?
- ❑ experienced problems at home?
- ❑ experienced actual personal or professional abuse?
- ❑ experienced abuse on your social networks?
- ❑ lost your sex drive?
- ❑ lost your appetite? Or gained weight?
- ❑ felt restless and irritable?
- ❑ experienced persistent headaches, stomach or back aches, muscle or joint pains?
- ❑ had difficulty falling asleep, staying asleep, or getting up in the morning?
- ❑ consumed more alcohol than usual?
- ❑ taken more mood-altering substances than usual?
- ❑ engaged in risky behaviour?
- ❑ engaged in self-harm?

David M Hinds

capacity for a range of emotions including depression. It's a natural part of our evolution and it is not a cause for shame. Depression is not your fault. But you can learn how to see it off. As indeed you are starting to do right now by reading this book.

A common factor when depressed clients showed up for the first time at my stress management consultancy in Milton Keynes (I'm no longer in practice now; I'm retired) was shame: the feeling of being weak or inadequate in some way, inferior, worthless, unlovable or unforgivable. Sometimes I would get the impression that a prospective client was beating himself or herself up mentally as they arrived for the initial consultation. In fact every single one of them was brave and wise in seeking help to overcome their problem.

The good news is that our own thoughts can play a major role in helping us to beat depression and this is one of many areas of therapy that we shall be concentrating on. Later, when you are ready, we are going to prepare ourselves for one of the essential keys to release from depression, which is to use a system of revised thought patterning.

I can assure you from my many years of working with depressed and highly-stressed clients, that you will find my methods easy to grasp, and highly rewarding. In essence, what we shall be doing in the latter part of the book is refashioning your brain with therapeutic thought patterns to beat depression based on the well proven principles of neuroscience.

Incidentally, the refashioning of your brain bit is actually quite simple. It turns out that the brain, all one hundred billion neurons of it, the most complex entity known to man, responds to refashioning according to basic instructions. All that is required is the correct instructions, which you will find in these pages, together with focused attention followed by dedicated practice.

Understandably, when we are depressed, we can make the mistake of assuming that our feelings are at fault, when the real problem is the way we have evolved. Many of us, particularly those who are depressed, have a tendency to blame ourselves for everyday events that happen and to put the worst possible interpretation on things that are said to us. This misguided and rather selective way of thinking is self-defeating and further fuels our feelings of low self-esteem and depression.

To get better quickly and to enjoy life to the full, I will teach you how to adopt the neuroscientific way of thinking which is forward-looking and positive. In order to differentiate between the two ways of thinking, we shall call the old way 'outmoded thinking' and the new way 'revised thinking'.

Fortunately, mastering this revised way of thinking is easier than you could possibly imagine at this early stage in the book. Everything required for success is included in the chapters to come. A major purpose of *Beat Depression* is to help readers to look at their individual circumstances and to develop the frame of mind necessary to break out of the depressive state. Once mastered, those skills will serve you well for a lifetime. In effect, you will have succeeded in refashioning your brain for your own immediate and future mental health benefit. You are less likely to suffer depression in the future because you will possess the mindset and the skills to deal with life's ups and downs.

3

'I cannot help myself'

THE MIND IS ITS OWN PLACE,
AND IN ITSELF CAN MAKE HEAVEN OF HELL,
A HELL OF HEAVEN.

—John Milton, *Paradise Lost*

The motivation to help oneself is simply *not there*.

The title of this chapter and the 'bottom line' are neither practical nor inspirational; they are defeatist. Why? The depressed person knows why. But family members, friends and loved ones, unless they have suffered the misery of clinical depression themselves, cannot understand why their well-meaning and genuine attempts to give comfort and help are sometimes ineffectual.

According to statistics released in 2017 by the World Health Organization, there has been a global increase in the number of people living with depression, up 18.4% since 2005, resulting in 322 million people being affected at any one time. The tragedy of depressive illness is that it can creep up without you realising and envelop you in a thickening cloud of energy-sapping misery, extinguishing almost all of the joys of living. No matter how intelligent or knowledgeable you may be, depression can at times make it difficult to help yourself or concentrate on even the simplest of tasks.

The mere fact that you are here with me now, sharing my experiences and reading this book, means that deep down you possess a courageous and determined streak that will help pull you through, even though you may be experiencing your darkest hour right now.

I am no stranger to depression. In my teens I was hospitalised for ten weeks with clinical depression. In the 1980s and 1990s, when I was treating clients suffering from depression in my own stress management consultancy, I thought my own problem was history. *Wrong!* In common with 50% of all stroke patients, I suffered a period of depression after partially recovering from two paralysing strokes, the second one, major, which occurred in the mid-1990s.

I have been where you are now. I know the territory.

And I'm happier now that I have been in my entire working career. While still recovering from stroke in the late 1990s, I met the woman who would later become my wife. Now, as I write, having this year celebrated our twenty-first wedding anniversary, I can honestly state that we love each other more with every passing year than in the heady days of our courting. But I digress… Let's get back to *your* forthcoming recovery.

Please bear in mind that a sense of deep isolation is an almost inevitable feature of depression. Difficulty in communicating with other people, even loved ones, makes you feel as though there is an impenetrable barrier between you and the rest of the world. This book is a medium of communication. It is for you to decide the pace and timing with which you respond to my ideas and experience.

I fully understand that you may be lacking in motivation right now, possibly feeling fragile in the extreme and perhaps unable to make any substantial effort to help yourself. In view of this, ***the very nature of your condition***, I will endeavour to make your recovery as painless and as easy to manage as possible.

5

Depression can break your heart

DEPRESSION IS A RISK FACTOR FOR HEART DISEASE. STUDIES
SHOW THAT HEART-ATTACK PATIENTS WHO ARE DEPRESSED
ARE MORE LIKELY TO DIE DURING THE FOLLOW-UP PERIOD.
—Frasure-Smith, Lesperance and Talajie

Research carried out over in the United States of America on behalf
of the National Institute of Mental Health and the National Heart,
Lung and Blood Institute has shown that depression and heart
disease are common companions. What is worse, each can lead to
the other.

It now appears that depression is an important risk factor for
heart disease along with high blood cholesterol and high blood
pressure. In a study conducted in Baltimore, it was found that of
1,551 people who underwent tests, those who were depressed were
four times more likely to have a heart attack in the next fourteen
years than those who were not. While researchers in Montreal found
that heart patients who were depressed were four times as likely to
die in the following six months than those who were not depressed.

The first studies of heart disease and depression showed that
people with heart disease were more depressed than healthy people.
While about one in six people have an episode of major depression in their lifetime, the ratio goes up to one in two for people
with heart disease. A study of individuals who were monitored
after experiencing a heart attack indicates that those who became

depressed after their heart attack are more at risk (Frasure-Smith, Lesperance and Talajie).

A large-scale study of European workers who had both depression and chronic medical problems found that when over time the depression improved, physical functioning also improved, as measured by there being fewer days spent in bed and less restriction on work and social life (Von Korff, Ormel, Katon and Lin).

How can depression lead to heart disease?

There is an ever-increasing weight of evidence to suggest that the presence of a major depressive disorder can suppress the body's immune system. Psychological distress may cause rapid heartbeat, high blood pressure, and faster blood clotting. It can also lead to elevated insulin and cholesterol levels. These risk factors, together with obesity, form a pattern of symptoms and often serve as a predictor of, and a response to, heart disease. Depressed individuals may feel slowed down and still have high levels of stress hormones. This can increase the work of the heart. When such individuals find themselves in highly stressful situations, the body's metabolism is diverted away from the type of tissue repair needed to combat heart disease.

All this makes for depressing reading, but already you have demonstrated a willingness to improve your personal healthcare by the simple act of reading this book. Very soon you will discover not only how to beat depression, but also how to reduce your risk of associated complications.

Exercise, of course, is a major protective factor against heart disease. In observational studies, exercise has been related to fewer depressive symptoms and it is beneficial and supremely therapeutic for those who are already depressed.

Fancy a break before moving on to the next chapter? What about a brisk walk or, if outdoors does not appeal, some press-ups, as many as you can comfortably manage?

6

'You mean I don't have to feel like this?'

IF A MAN WILL BEGIN WITH CERTAINTIES, HE SHALL
END IN DOUBTS; BUT IF HE WILL BE CONTENT TO BEGIN
WITH DOUBTS, HE SHALL END IN CERTAINTIES.
—Francis Bacon, The Advancement of Learning

You have the power today to choose how you will feel. This book will give you the means to use that power.

With the major advances that have been made in medicine today and our greater understanding of brain chemistry and therapy for the mind, it is no longer necessary to wait for depression to lift. You can take simple steps to start the process right now. The first step, which I trust you have already taken, or are about to take, is to consult your doctor and get the professionals working for you.

There are six steps to complete recovery and by the end of this chapter, you will be ready for the second step, which is to establish why you may have become depressed in the first place. As we progress to Part Three, you will learn to recognise and identify your particular state of depression so that you can familiarise yourself with the warning signs and take steps to avoid them in future.

Part Four is rather like a set of tools or a make-up kit—the basic essentials you will need to use or apply to bring about your recovery. In Part Five, you should be in a position to ease the gloom by engaging in one or more of the therapies that appeal to you from the range on offer. In Part Six, the final step in beating depression, you will have the opportunity to rediscover the joy of living.

Throughout the book, the central theme is for getting better from all variations of depressive illness, namely the need to quit outmoded thinking in favour of revised thinking. To make this realisable for everyone, from a child to a pensioner, I have packaged the process into easy stages.

Depression means different things to different people. This book contains a full range of therapies available to a depressed person. Clearly, not all will apply to any one individual and you will be free to choose which are most appropriate to you and your condition.

A vital ingredient for your recovery is hope. Perhaps at this moment you feel recovery is beyond you. I will not ask you at this stage to be confident of recovery, but I ask you to hope for recovery.

'You can't massacre an idea, you cannot run tanks over hope,' said Ronald Reagan, fortieth president of the United States.

You have the power today to choose how you will feel. With hope in your ability to recover from depression, this book will give you the means to use that power as we progress to the therapeutic stages to come.

PART TWO

Why Me?

7

Inherited genes

WHAT LIES BEHIND US, AND WHAT LIES BEFORE US ARE
TINY MATTERS, COMPARED TO WHAT LIES WITHIN US.
—Ralph Waldo Emerson

We have no choice but to make the best of who we are.

There is a genetic predisposition to some forms of depression, particularly those that recur. For instance, it has been established that if one identical twin suffers from depression, there is a 70 per cent chance that the other twin will also. Non-identical twins, in common with other relatives, parents or children of a person who suffer from depression, run a 25 per cent risk of depressive illness due to the genetic factor.

The genetic factor appears to be an important one. Researchers on both sides of the Atlantic identified two groups of adopted individuals—those who had been diagnosed as having a depressive illness and those who did not suffer from depression. They found that the biological relatives of adopted persons with depressive illnesses had higher rates of clinical (major) depressive illnesses than did relatives of those who were not depressed.

How is it that our brains can be affected by the genetic factor to render some of us more vulnerable to depression than others?

People who have a greater biological sensitivity to depression than others are more likely to switch into depressed states of mind because something goes wrong with the way that neurochemicals are produced and used in the brain. This malfunction is believed to be due to our genes, the segments of DNA that control a vast number of chemical processes.

Genes are essential for life. They control the colour and texture of our skin, the face, the figure, the colour of our eyes and hair, and they bring about changes and developments within ourselves so that, as we grow, our sexual organs develop. Genes also play a part in personality and susceptibility to certain types of illnesses, including depression, but our individuality and the type of person we become mostly depends on ourselves and how we interpret the experiences we have had during infancy and early childhood.

The way the brain develops during infancy and early childhood depends very much on social input. The brain of a child who is loved and wanted might mature differently from that of a child who is abused and constantly threatened. Our actual real-life experiences condition the brain and this aspect of development marries what we perceive is happening to us in the outside world with what is going on inside our heads.

This may sound fine in theory. But how does it work in practice? At the fundamental cell level, a human brain might be compared to a computer. After all, computers are essentially a series of tiny switches that can be programmed for either 'on' or 'off', depending on the task to be performed. Likewise, our brain cells (neurons, to be more precise) either 'fire', discharging an electrochemical signal for some kind of action to take place *(run*—Daddy is mad at you), or 'do not fire', if no change is required (don't run—Mummy wants to give you a sweetie).

When, as an infant, you were distressed (as in the first bracketed example above), your brain chemistry changed to prepare you for the ordeal at hand, arousing tension in the body. Hormones such as adrenalin, noradrenalin, cortisol, and a number of different chemicals, impact together to affect the way transmission takes place in the brain.

Over time, and with repetition, these significant chemical changes, which occur in response to what is happening to us in the outside world, can have the effect of modifying our brain receptors and the kind of attachment that one nerve cell makes with another. There is a connection between the shaping of our infant brain and the outside world right from our very early experiences of life.

But what can we do to beat depression *now*?

Let's start with what we should avoid doing: we should not blame our parents for the less than perfect set of genes we inherited, or for the less than perfect upbringing we experienced as a child, even if our experiences were downright miserable. We can't change the past and our genes (some of which will be rather good and better than other people's) cannot be part-exchanged or re-engineered.

Blaming others for our predicament is one of the surest ways to stay in depression. In blaming one or other of our parents or anyone else involved in our upbringing, *including ourselves*, we negate our power as individuals and render ourselves vulnerable.

The future is decided by our current thinking. In order to break free from depression, it is imperative to believe that our parents or guardians were trying to do the best they could with the limited understanding, awareness and knowledge they had at the time. If there is something that you need to forgive them for, but you don't quite know how to go about it, you may find the perfect solution for you as we progress through the therapy sessions later.

The finest contribution to future happiness that can be made by the damaged child, cheated of his or her own childhood, and now in adulthood, is to ensure that the mistakes of previous generations are not allowed to manifest themselves in future generations.

8

Bitter thoughts

IF WE COULD READ THE SECRET HISTORY OF OUR ENEMIES,
WE SHOULD FIND IN EACH MAN'S LIFE SORROW AND SUFFERING
ENOUGH TO DISARM HOSTILITY.
—Henry Wadsworth Longfellow, Driftwood

Forgive and forget.

Of all the quotations in this book, and I believe there are no fewer than sixty-seven excellent ones, the one from Longfellow is the most telling of all. I am fortunate in that these days I have many friends and very few enemies. On those rare occasions when I look into the eyes of someone who regards me as the enemy, I remember Longfellow's words.

In contrast to many the times in the past when I was prone to depression, I am no longer prepared to entertain bitter thoughts. I know, from experience, such thoughts do more damage to me than anyone else.

At strategic points throughout this book, in very small, gentle stages, you and I must work together to banish bitter thoughts from your mind and to establish a comfortable and forgiving environment so that you feel less inclined to embrace bitterness in the future.

It would be dishonest and unrealistic of me to think that I could teach you the techniques necessary to make this possible in

David M Hinds

one short (or extended) chapter. I can't. There are many seemingly unrelated matters we must deal with along the way before you can be expected to grasp that coming to terms with your past, and quitting outmoded thinking in favour of revised thinking, is the key to permanent release from depression.

Happily, we can deal with all of these matters within the pages of this book and we shall do so with considerable respect to your sensitivities. Before we can make great progress, however, we need to examine our own bitter thoughts and observe how we are keeping our suffering alive, red-hot and self-destructive.

All too often we perpetuate our pain by keeping it the focus of our thoughts, replaying our hurts over and over again in our minds, magnifying our injustices and vilifying the perceived offender in the process. We frequently add to our discomfort by being overly sensitive and reacting out of all proportion to minor irritations and temporary setbacks. How many of us have punished ourselves time and time again by taking things too personally?

Learning to exercise more control over our thought processes, and finding ways to neutralise our bitter thoughts, will give our brain chemistry a chance to recover from the ravages of yesteryear. Once we have mastered this simple procedure, we can heal the wounds of the distant or recent past and depression will lift because our thoughts play a powerful role in deciding whether or not we become or remain depressed.

How can this be? Quite simply, because our thoughts (those ugly, bitter ones, and any others you may care to have) come *before* the process of chemical change takes place in our brains.

We shall leave the mechanics of how we can train our minds to be more selective with our thoughts in general, and less generous with our bitter thoughts in particular, until you are feeling up to the challenge. For the moment, the all-important factor to embrace is that depression tends to sidetrack our thoughts and engulf them in one of seven downward-spiralling thought patterns. I have a tendency to refer to these undesirable thoughts as the seven bittermints, because I don't like mints. It would be a tremendous breakthrough in your recovery, and I would be so proud of you, if you were to feel able to identify your particular thought pattern from the seven bittermints below. If you think that more than one applies to you, select the predominant one. We will address your findings later.

The seven bittermints

1. **Unlovability**—e.g. my boyfriend/girlfriend/partner/ date/that handsome stranger, etc. dumped me/ doesn't love me/doesn't want to know me. I am unlovable. No one will ever love me again.

2. **Inferiority**—e.g. my parents didn't care for me/I was abused/ abandoned/imprisoned/terrorised/they wouldn't let me join the club/nobody likes me/I have no education/no money/job/ friends/home/prospects/ sexual prowess, etc. I will never be as good as others.

3. **Entrapment**—e.g. I feel trapped by my family/ child/partner/ job/circumstances/age/state of health/ environment, etc. I can't do what I want to do.

4. **Failure**—e.g. I didn't make the grade/pass the exam/get the place at university/get the job/win the contest. I was demoted/sidelined/fired/made redundant. My business/investment /plan/ operation/ expedition failed, etc. I am a complete failure.

5. **Inadequacy**—e.g. I am unable to cope with new situations/the new company posting/the new job/the new house/the arrival of my baby/the rumour that is going around about me. I feel unworthy and despondent because I cannot provide what is expected of me.

6. **Loneliness**—e.g. I am all alone in the world now and I would like someone to care/talk to/get to know/

the right-hand reel of tape (your future without depression using strategies that will work for you). Later, in Parts Four, Five and Six of the book, we have some unfinished business on the left-hand reel (your past) to sort out. In the meantime, let's ease our more immediate anxieties passing through the tape head with an excursion to Paradise Beach.

Paradise Beach

First, read the rest of this chapter. Then relax, take off your shoes and close your eyes. Become aware of your breathing and give yourself a few moments to settle.

Keep your eyes closed, but imagine what you could see if you were to open them. Fix your mind on just one object in the room with which you are familiar and explore its shape ... its texture... its contours.

Imagine this object melting in front of your eyes without warmth or danger. Imagine it dissolving into white sand, crumbling under its own weight and becoming an assemblage of sand. Be aware that everything around your object is also crumbling into sand until you are left lying or sitting on an expanse of shimmering, white sand.

You are on Paradise Beach ... a beach of soft, white sand. Towering behind you are palm trees gently swaying in the breeze. In front of you is the crystal-clear sea. You can hear the water lapping the beach and feel the warmth of the sun on your skin. There is a slight breeze keeping you at a constant safe and comfortable temperature.

Be aware of the sky above you with its fluffy, cotton wool clouds passing overhead and away to the horizon. Feel your muscles relax and become more flexible as you lie or sit on this beautiful island where you are alone and undisturbed. You are happy under the sun and enjoying the peace and quiet of solitude with only the birds to keep you company. Above the sounds of the sea, listen to the far-off cries of seagulls and experience the bliss of freedom from all your cares and worries.

If you want to, you can move into the water and feel the gentle waves pulsating against your ankles. Feel the sun penetrate your body, reaching deep into your bones, loosening all your ligaments and tendons, filling you with a warm sensation, calming and relaxing you.

Now prepare yourself to leave this place and come back to reality. Keep your eyes closed. Take a last look around you, firmly stamping whatever you see on your consciousness, so that you can easily return here whenever you wish. Slowly become aware of the sand around you reverting back into the shape of the object you originally fixed your mind upon. Without opening your eyes, visualise the rest of the room you are in. When you feel ready, gently stretch your body and open your eyes. You are calmer and more relaxed than you were before.

Say the following words to yourself with conviction, they will become true and relevant to you as you repeat this exercise once a day for thirty days.

> 'I am feeling calmer and more relaxed; physically, I will begin to feel stronger and more capable. I will gain more confidence and because of this feeling of confidence which 1 can feel in my very fingertips, I will be able to face things more easily. I will be able to do all of the things I need to do. 'I will feel this confidence welling up inside me and I will feel rested *and* relaxed. *I* will find it easier to concentrate and as *I* do so, *I* will feel *a* deep sense of security *and* comfort. *I* will find that my thoughts are less centred upon myself and as each day goes past, I will feel stronger in my mind and in my body.'

10

Losing in love

THERE ARE TWO TRAGEDIES IN LIFE.
One is to lose your heart's desire. The other is to gain it.
—George Bernard Shaw, Man and Superman

Losing in love hurts like hell and is almost guaranteed to induce anger, depression and despair. You may feel that you will never love, or be loved, again. You will, of course, but you cannot be expected to believe this for a while yet. The overwhelming sense of shock, outrage, disbelief, and heart-rending grief at losing your lover defies all rational thought. It shatters the very bedrock of your emotions.

This experience will humble us and we must learn to accept that it will take a while before we can get back on top and start living again. We are emotionally damaged and—just as if we had met with an accident and were physically wounded—it will take time for the healing process to take effect. In the meantime, we must take care of ourselves because we are fragile. We need special treats and plenty of sleep. In fact, we need and deserve an army of helpers. The time has come to be supported by our friends, who are so important they merit a chapter of their own later in this book.

Don't feel bad because you need your friends to help you now as never before. What are friends for? They are not only there to share the good times with you, as your real friends will be delighted to demonstrate. Just remember how good you felt the last time you helped someone in need. Surely you would encourage your friends to call on you if they were suffering as you are now? I, for one, am not too proud to admit that my closest and most treasured friends have seen me and comforted me in the depths of my despair.

Having been ravaged by two strokes and very badly treated by a woman—I think even she would agree with that—I believe that we benefit more from the painful experiences of life than we do from the periods of ecstasy. I was hurting as you are hurting now and, despite the apparent impossibility at the time, I have found the woman of my dreams and we are supremely happy. You will learn much about beating depression and overcoming the trials of life in this book. No matter how unlikely the prospect of future love and happiness might seem to you right now, I would expect you to be in a position to surprise yourself before too long.

In the meantime, since you're hurting so much already, I have no qualms about introducing you to yet more pain—aversion therapy—in the form of a rubber band to be worn around the wrist at all times, day and night. Make no mistake; used correctly, the humble rubber band is one of the big guns of stress management when it comes to getting absent lovers out of your life for ever more. Make sure it fits loosely enough not to restrict circulation, but snugly enough so it won't fall off. Every time you think of your ex, snap the rubber band! Snap it firmly so that it stings, but not hard enough to leave welts on your wrist.

This type of aversion therapy might seem crazy but it works. How does it work? Your subconscious mind quickly comes to associate the twang of pain from the rubber band with thoughts of the offending ex-lover. Your subconscious mind will, over time, short circuit the thought process to avoid the pain. Thoughts of your ex become less and less frequent and soon it will be time to cast off the rubber band and celebrate your new-found freedom with champagne and friends.

11

Career crash

IT'S A RECESSION WHEN YOUR NEIGHBOUR LOSES HIS
JOB; IT'S A DEPRESSION WHEN YOU LOSE YOURS.
—*Harry S. Truman*

There is always another opportunity... After two strokes, I know this to be true.

For just about everyone, losing a job or experiencing a career crash can be a shattering and soul-destroying experience. For many people, however, once the initial shock has worn off, it can be a golden (forced, unexpected, probably inconvenient, but nevertheless there for the taking) opportunity to demonstrate the strength of their character. As a direct result of misfortune or, in some cases, foul play by employers, millions of people the world over have found satisfaction in self-employment or been motivated to seek that special job that they might otherwise never have striven for.

Everyone recovers from depression unless, of course, one throws in the towel while gripped in the depths of despair. It might seem all-embracing while it has you in its clutches but depression, however frightening, is never permanent. Many people, when they beat it and return to the real world, are supercharged with energy and determination to change their lives for the better. This is the reason why we shall have more fun and make accelerated progress as we graduate to the second half of this book.

Think back to your schooldays. The general idea was to learn your lessons in class first and then be tested later. In the university of life things often appear to be the other way around. We are all tested at some time or other—during a career crisis or a bout of depression, perhaps—before a learning curve follows, when we have both the opportunity and a vested interest in learning our lessons so that we can end up benefiting greatly from our present predicament.

Hopefully, you are already on my wavelength because you are several chapters into the book that is going to help you to get things right. Here are some useful questions to ask yourself and to discuss with your family and friends. Be aware that your first reaction may be to dismiss the questions. It is not your first reaction that I am interested in; it is your second, third and subsequent thoughts that count. It is your considered opinion that I am after, and I know how difficult it is for you to give this when you are depressed.

- How many different ways are there in which I could plausibly end up benefiting from my present predicament?

- Have I failed if I benefit from the experience and move my life forwards? Are there any circumstances in which one day I could conceivably say, 'I'm glad this happened to me' or 'This is the best thing that ever happened to me'?

- Believe it or not, I can honestly say that the major stroke I suffered in 1995 was ultimately beneficial to me. OK, so it took me five years to make a complete recovery, but this tragedy forced me to review my life and change my ways for the better. I'm happy now.

David M Hinds

12

Alcohol, smoking cessation, and vaping

OF COURSE YOU CAN GET A QUART INTO A PINT POT—YOU CAN GET A COUPLE OF GALLONS INTO IT, IF YOU STAY UNTIL CLOSING TIME.

—Patrick Skene Catling

All things in moderation or not at all.

These days, there is renewed acceptance that some alcoholic drinks—when consumed in moderation—may have a part to play in health and nutrition. There can be no doubt, however, that heavy drinking and alcoholism can cause depression, serious illness and death. Sensible alcohol consumption to release inhibitions and to help get the conversation flowing at parties, etc. can, of course, be beneficial, but some of us may be tempted to drink to excess to relieve a depressed mood or to 'drown our sorrows' and that can be dangerous.

Some people who are depressed and lacking in energy may use alcohol to help them keep going and cope with life. This might seem sensible to the depressed person but will prove to be a short-lived solution because any benefits from alcohol soon wear off and excessive drinking can so easily become a habit. Furthermore, there is evidence that changes in brain chemistry produced by excess alcohol increase the likelihood of further depression.

In view of the fact that many doctors who have questioned patients about their drinking habits believe that most people underestimate their alcohol consumption by as much as fifty per cent, I would urge you to adopt the sound medical advice outlined below.

- Avoid the temptation of using alcohol as a means of drowning your sorrows or lifting your spirits.
- Seek immediate help from Alcoholics Anonymous if you get frequent hangovers, along with the shakes, that are 'cured' by yet another drink.
- Get into the habit of sipping your drinks slowly and substitute every other drink with a non-alcoholic drink.
- Do not drink on an empty stomach.
- If you are hosting a party or an event, be considerate; offer non-alcoholic drinks as well as alcohol.
- Ask your doctor or pharmacist if it is safe to drink with any medicine that you have been prescribed.
- Give your vital organs a break. Have at least two or three days a week when you do not drink alcohol at all.

Excessive drinking actually *leads* to depression more often than it is a *symptom* of depression. If you have difficulty cutting down or knowing when to stop, total abstinence may be the only sustainable option. Many former alcoholics have found happiness without booze, but not before they recognised that they had a problem with alcohol.

Smoking cessation

Quitting smoking is difficult enough when you're feeling happy. Unfortunately, it can become further challenging due to depression—a common complaint early on in smoking cessation. Nicotine withdrawal is the primary reason for periods of depression that some people experience when quitting smoking. This is because your brain becomes dependent on nicotine as it bonds with your brain's receptors to trigger the release of dopamine, which is known as the *feel-good* hormone.

Once you stop smoking and produce less dopamine than your mind and body have become accustomed to, low mood and depressed feelings can often result. The important thing to remember here is that these sensations are merely temporary. The longer you abstain from smoking, the quicker your mood and feelings get back to normal. Quitting smoking is a major lifestyle change—a very worthwhile one—and the best way to counter the dopamine deprivation is to get out for quick, frequent walks. Fresh air is always invigorating and exercise releases endorphins in the brain, which invariably improves mood.

During the course of quitting smoking, body and mind are in a state of flux and transition, and it's only to be expected that new ex-smokers struggle with their emotions. Your mind will soon balance and benefit from this new healthy state of affairs.

Sadly, many would-be tobacco quitters fall into the mega-trap of the century set by the big tobacco companies of vaping. Governments and national health departments the world over, including Public Health England, have allowed themselves to be suckered by the major players in the industry into cautiously welcoming vaping because it is considerably less harmful than smoking.

The fly in the ointment here is that vaping is nicotine addiction and nicotine is a poison harmful to the human body. In January 2019 the London Evening Standard reported that e-cigarette users were seeking help in increasing numbers to quit vaping. This, at a time when the impact of marketing has made vaping appear to be a lifestyle choice.

How many people—*if the true facts were presented to them*—would choose to poison themselves with a substance that, drop for drop, is more toxic than rattlesnake venom?

Quitting smoking and breaking free from nicotine addiction—which means no vaping, otherwise you remain a nicotine addict—

bring with it a tremendous sense of pride and empowerment. Successful quitters can take comfort in knowing that millions of people have been through this sometimes painful process successfully before them. Many, including me, subsequently reported that quitting was among the most rewarding and beneficial experiences of their lives.

If your depression is brought on solely by the act of quitting, press on until you reach your goal of being nicotine free and then your mood should lift through natural causes.

The best advice I can give to any potential quitter—*and when I was in practice, clients used to pay me rather a lot of money for it*—is, simply refrain from putting a cigarette or vaping device in your mouth. Don't even allow yourself the luxury of thinking about it. Think about something else. Do something else. And then the moment of temptation will have passed and you are one step closer to your goal. Aids of any kind are worthless. Willpower is what you need and money can't buy it but persistence and determination can conjure it up free, even to the weakest of souls.

If your depression is deeper and more complex, then press on until you reach your goal of successfully quitting, and keep right on reading this book because there are exciting therapies ahead that will ensure that you beat depression.

A double win for you!

13

All alone?

> On stage I make love to 25,000 people;
> then I go home alone.
>
> —Janis Joplin

Never give up hope on love.

The difference between enjoying the luxury, the independence and the freedom of being alone, and being lonely, is essentially a matter of how we feel about the experience of actually being on our own. Being alone by choice is beneficial to the soul; being lonely can be soul-destroying because it feels as if you are stranded in your own private world where only you speak the language and know the customs. You can see other people, you can hear their voices, but you don't seem to be able to relate to them and that hurts. It is humiliating.

When you don't bond with anyone else and can't remember the last time you shared an intimate look with another human being, you begin to feel the pain of emptiness and abandonment. If you don't have someone in your life who cares, what incentive is there for you to get up in the morning and do your best?

Perpetual loneliness can result in shame and self-neglect and eventually you start to wonder if there really is anyone in this world who will love and cherish you.

Almost everyone knows that dreadful sensation of being with people and, at the same time, experiencing devastating loneliness.

There are many possible reasons why we feel isolated and alone when, in reality, we are not.

Of all the symptoms of depression, the sense of being isolated and cut off from the rest of humanity must surely be the cruellest. On the other hand, all the lonely people who John Lennon and Paul McCartney were referring to in their song 'Eleanor Rigby' were surely not *all* depressed *all of the time*? Some of them may simply not have had a partner with whom to share their lives.

I recognise the paralysing effect of loneliness and how it can impede recovery from depression. I shall help you through this difficult period in Part Four. The chapter 'Greater self-esteem', in particular, may be useful to you, but don't be tempted to rush ahead to it now. There is valuable information you need to pick up along the way first. In the meantime, please believe that loneliness is a problem for many people and it is conquerable. We shall conquer it. A chance meeting with a former secretary of mine certainly provided information helpful to me.

When I had been a partner in a magazine publishing house, my secretary was the most valuable member of my team. Whenever I walked into the office, she would immediately decipher my mood and determine, as she smiled and said, 'Good morning', whether or not that moment was the right one to present me with any bad news or tricky assignments. I always held her in high esteem (as indeed I still do), and several years after selling my interest in the business, I stepped out of a cab and there she was…

It was lunchtime, so naturally we headed straight for the nearest pub and got ourselves up-to-date with all the latest news and gossip. Just as we were about to leave, I couldn't resist the urge to ask her what she thought of me as a boss! At first she tried a touch of subtle diplomacy to side-step the question. I persisted, confident in my mind that working for me had been the happiest five years of her working life. Being me, I just had to hear it from her lips!

15

Social Media

DON'T SAY ANYTHING ONLINE THAT YOU WOULDN'T WANT
PLASTERED ON A BILLBOARD WITH YOUR FACE ON IT.

—Erin Bury

Many of us live with the uneasy feeling that we—*and our children*—spend too much time using our phones and laptops. The obvious question is what should we do about it?

The answer, according to doctors at the United Kingdom's Royal College of Paediatrics and Child Health (RCPCH), is that children shouldn't look at their screens within an hour of going to bed, and parents should set a good example by keeping their own screen time under control.

In the RCPCH Screen Time Guidance document, Doctor Max Davie, the co-author of the report, says, "Parents should ask themselves whether family screen use is under control, and whether children are getting enough sleep and exercise to be healthy and happy."

The latest research indicates that children with a daily screen time of more than two hours tend to have more depressive symptoms, according to the RCPCH, and yet a study showed that the average iPhone user put picked it up eighty times a day! A further study in the United States revealed that fifty-one per cent of teenagers felt their parents were distracted by their phones when having conversations.

Social media has dramatically changed the way we communicate, socialise and make and maintain friendships. While there are major benefits to be had by dipping into your digital world from time to time, there are tremendous risks in living your life in a social media dependent world.

It's much easier to tap in harsh statements on a keyboard with no physical face-to-face contact and no immediate consequences than it is to communicate on the street or in a social or family setting. Disjointed shorthand conversations frequently result in misunderstandings and it doesn't help that digital communication occurs at a rapid pace, one that is difficult to control and fully process at times.

A report on social media and mental health published in the UK by the Royal Society for Public Health surveyed fifteen hundred young people aged between fourteen and twenty-four to determine the effects of social media on the subject of depression, anxiety self-esteem and body image. The Royal Society's findings concluded that YouTube actually had a positive effect on mental health, while Facebook, Twitter, Instagram and Snapchat all had negative effects on mental health.

University of Pennsylvania researchers discovered that students who drastically cut time spent on Facebook, Instagram and Snapchat experienced 'significant declines' in symptoms associated with depression. Psychologist Melissa G Hunt, the report's lead author, said, "It is ironic, but perhaps not surprising that reducing social media, which promised to help us connect with others, actually helps people feel less lonely and depressed." One participant in the survey said, "Not comparing my life to the lives of others had a much stronger impact than I expected, and I felt a lot more positive about myself during those weeks when my access to social media was limited to ten minutes per day."

The evidence is mounting to support the link between social media and depression in young children, teens and young adults.

There can be a tremendous loss of self-esteem—*especially in teenage girls*—when they compare themselves negatively with artificially improved and professionally presented images of those who appear to be prettier, thinner more popular and richer.

David Rosenberg, Professor of Psychiatry and Neuroscience at Wayne State University, reports that social media and technology can be dangerous. "Excessive use of each tends to engender impaired social interactions and an increased sense of isolation. It can also foster a certain competition between one's real life and one's virtual life. That is, a tug-of-war between being engrossed in posting experiences on social media, sending texts and taking selfies instead of enjoying the moment for what it's worth."

At the other end of the scale, incidents of cyber-related bullying is sadly on the increase. While adults can frequently be vulnerable to this modern-day variant of bullying, it is young children and teenagers who are most at risk. To a large extent, however, the psychological damage caused by bullying is preventable. My favourite quote on the subject is from the famous United States First Lady, Eleanor Roosevelt. She said these famous words long before the Internet was invented:

"No one can make you feel inferior without your consent."

Just think about the poignant meaning of those words for a moment and how apt they are today in this age of rising suicides.

The indications are that mental health generally has deteriorated across the developed world and untreated cases of depression have risen sharply during the Covid-19 epidemic. Even further, post-Covid! The Russian invasion of Ukraine, plus the aftermath of the Speaker of the United States House of Representatives, Nancy Pelosi's visit to Taiwan and China's reaction will, in my view, contribute to further instability in the world and even more cases of depression will result.

Another indicator of the state of modern-day life is the internet and the internet itself needs multi-government action around the world to compel the media and tech giants to fully accept their responsibilities.

Although some governments are beginning to pay lip service to the problem, the reality is that it's left to you and me to put right the damage caused by depression. We'll do it. By the time we're done on the last page of the book, you will come out of this depressive episode stronger than you were at the outset. Our efforts, yours and mine together, will set you up well for the rest of your life. All those malicious or discouraging Facebook posts can be made to metaphorically bounce off the walls of your confidence if you take on board the words of Eleanor Roosevelt from the previous page.

And now it's time to hear from her husband, the 32nd President of the United States of America…

dominant partner can be satisfying and beneficial to both parties. However, problems arise if one partner is led to believe that he or she must behave in a certain manner. The submissive partner, craving the approval of the other, seeks to live up to the dominant partner's expectations and may end up feeling inadequate and depressed if approval is not forthcoming.

Over many years of treating depressed clients in my UK consultancy, I have discovered that if ever a case of clinical depression roller-coasted—that is to say, the client's condition improved, but then relapsed—the reason was most likely to be contact with a forceful personality.

How can a dominant personality adversely affect someone's condition to the point of relapse?

To find both the answer and subsequent release from the rollercoaster phenomenon in depression, we may have to gently but persistently probe the depressed person's background and upbringing, as well as his or her current and recent relationships, in order to stimulate recognition and identification of the relevant dominant personality. Once this problem is out in the open it is relatively straightforward to deal with.

STEP 1: Think
Remind yourself who the influential people in your life are.

STEP 2: The process of elimination
Make a complete list of all the people who have opposed you in any way, commencing with the most recent opposition, and then continuing right back to childhood. For example, a typical list might read: husband/wife, ex-partner, VAT inspector, bank manager, boss, landlord/landlady, uncle/aunt, doctor, father, mother, teacher, nanny. It could be that the list includes someone now dead.

Go through the list *deleting only one entry at a time*, commencing with the least influential and, therefore, the least likely to be unknowingly causing you problems. Repeat the process until *only one* name remains—there must be *only one*: the significant one. If there are ten names on the list to begin with, you must go through the process nine times in total.

STEP 3: Dealing with the problem once identified
Sometimes the significant one is no longer present in your life, for example, an overly strict stepmother or an institutional care worker. Tell yourself this person no longer has the right to exert his or her influence over you. You can do very well without their approval in future. Later, in Part Four of this book, you will discover powerful new techniques that will enable you to disconnect from the past and move ahead.

You should by now be in a position to recognise with absolute certainty the person who is adversely affecting your ability to recover from depression if, indeed, you are one of the minority of people to be emotionally impacted in this way.

In the event that you are still confused, bear in mind that this process can be even more effective if you get someone you respect to do it with you, to help you with your responses and to acknowledge your identification of the dominant personality. Run through the process again, this time with the assistance of an unbiased friend or relative. This person should *not* be the dominant personality.

If the significant dominant personality is currently part of your life you **must** make radical changes to the nature or status of the relationship in order to get well and stay that way. In the event that you are romantically attached to, or professionally connected with, this person, he or she must be willing to respond positively to your sensitivities in future or the relationship is doomed.

In a worst-case scenario, if you don't get the co-operation you need, you should possibly consider ending the relationship or, at the very least, taking an immediate, four-week break from it. Why twenty-eight days? That's how long, after a trauma like this, it will take for your mind to rest easy and regain equilibrium.

This is a difficult process and you should feel proud that you have identified the person responsible for your discomfort and been able to understand how he/she has influenced you. You have to ask yourself why you allow yourself to be tormented in this way. You must work on building up your self-esteem. Value yourself more than you have done before. It is your life.

18

Misadventure, debt or despondency

HE WHO HAS NEVER HOPED CAN NEVER DESPAIR.
—George Bernard Shaw, *Caesar and Cleopatra*

Do you have a friend or a colleague who can help? Anyone? Ask them for help! Otherwise this is the moment for the hero within you to shine.

Misadventure

A simple misadventure like moving home and finding out, when you get there, you don't like it, or, accepting a new job and then discovering, too late, that you hate it, can bring on depression unless you can see a way out of the situation: a means of putting things right. If you find yourself trapped, this is fertile ground for the onset of depression. This can easily happen if you allow other people to manipulate things to suit them. It can take a while to figure out that the new situation doesn't necessarily suit you. The obvious depression-free way out of this situation in the examples given above is to move or find a different job, but that could cost and lead you into debt.

Debt

Debt and money worries are a major cause of stress and depression and insufficient funds have wrecked many relationships and lives. Although having sufficient money to meet all demands doesn't totally eliminate stress, not having enough money to remain solvent is definitely stress inducing and liable to lead to depression.

Financial consultants recommend that we should save at least ten per cent of our earnings. Apparently, we will enjoy a clean bill of financial health for life if we spend what we have left over after saving rather than saving what's left over after spending! It is never too late to get into the habit of saving and even those on low incomes can usually make economies if really determined.

If you are already in debt, seek advice and guidance without delay from your lender or an independent agency. In the United Kingdom, the nationwide network of Citizens Advice Bureaux can be most helpful. Here are their suggestions to help avoid some of the classic causes of financial problems:

- Except for essentials, try to avoid shopping if you feel lonely, bored, stressed or depressed.
- Avoid shopping simply for recreation purposes. Find something potentially less expensive to do.
- Shop only with a shopping list in hand and stick to a prearranged spending budget.
- Give yourself a cooling-off period before making any non- essential purchases.
- Whenever you are tempted to buy anything that could be regarded as a luxury, work out in advance just how many hours you are going to have to work in order to be able to afford this item.
- Utilising this system, you may decide that you don't want to spend the money after all.

Despondency

Life for the clinically depressed, despondent person can seem like a life sentence of regret: regret for the lost opportunities and the mistakes of the past, regret for the momentum and enthusiasm that have evaporated from present-day life, and premature regret for a future perceived by the individual to be futile and already lost. Given this degree of despondency, it is hardly surprising that the depressed person's thoughts are permeated by feelings of self-doubt, lack of self-esteem and even self-loathing. But one of the great joys of my life has been seeing, participating in, and hearing about people like you turning their lives around using the solutions available in this book.

19

Death of a loved one

I KNOW FOR CERTAIN THAT WE NEVER LOSE
THE PEOPLE WE LOVE, EVEN TO DEATH.
THEY CONTINUE TO PARTICIPATE IN EVERY
ACT, THOUGHT AND DECISION WE MAKE.
THEIR LOVE LEAVES AN INDELIBLE IMPRINT IN
OUR MEMORIES. WE FIND COMFORT IN
KNOWING THAT OUR LIVES HAVE BEEN ENRICHED
BY HAVING SHARED THEIR LOVE.

—Leo Buscaglia

Death… This is when true friends show their worth. The death of a loved one can be the most awful thing to come to terms with. Grieving is a natural way to release emotional feelings and it is our traditional way of making peace with whomever has been taken away from us. The process takes time and cannot be rushed. Many people choose a period of solitude as their way of coming to terms with what has happened. For others, equally devastated by their loss, the comfort of others is what is needed.

Family and friends can help to keep depression at bay by spending time with the person who has been bereaved. It is not so much words of comfort that are needed at times like this, more the willingness to be with them during the time of their pain and distress. A sympathetic arm around their shoulders will express care and support when words are not enough.

Grief is a process of adaptation and passes through a number of recognisable stages. These stages include alarm, shock, denial, anger, guilt, acceptance and adjustment. People in mourning who become depressed are often having difficulty transcending the last two stages—acceptance and adjustment.

Touch can be instrumental in opening up the pathways to emotion and helping to release the anguish of grief. When we are trying to hold back painful emotions, we clench our muscles, locking in memories and thoughts that we have difficulty in dealing with. The professional touch of a masseur or a masseuse, in a relaxed and private environment, can have the effect of allowing blocked emotions to flow more freely.

The change of seasons can provide a change of focus and a turning point in your life. Even in the depths of winter we can see snowdrops rising from beneath the snow. If you have access to a small piece of soil and a few seeds, why not plant a miniature garden of remembrance? Many people find that growing new life while they're in mourning soaks up some of the pain associated with bereavement.

Guidelines to help you through the death of a loved one

- Accept that grief is normal and it can be a very deep type of pain.

- Expect to experience some or all of the various stages of grief.

- Remember that everyone grieves differently; in their own private way. There is no right or wrong way of grieving.

- It's normal to be in denial for a while after your loved one dies. Some people cry a lot, others might not be able to cry or show much emotion. Either way of grieving is perfectly okay and natural.

- After the reality of death sets in, you might feel angry. This is one of many passing emotions; another is guilt— *unearned guilt*—that some people experience. It will pass.

- There is invariably a feeling of deep sadness which can develop into depression.

- No matter how you may feel at the moment, you will come to accept the death of your loved one in the end.

- Return to your favourite activities when the time feels right or develop new ones.

- Life goes on and there are new experiences for you to embrace. You will be happy again. You will get over the death of your loved one.

PART THREE

States of Depression

20

Is this your child?

CHILDREN BEGIN BY LOVING THEIR PARENTS; AFTER A TIME
THEY JUDGE THEM; RARELY, IF EVER, DO THEY FORGIVE THEM.
—Oscar Wilde, *A Woman of No Importance*

A happy childhood for their offspring is the wish of every parent, but not the experience of every child. It is unrealistic to expect a child, particularly a young one, to say, 'I am depressed'. In fact, the child who is truly sad is unlikely to be able to ask for help in any language that those in a position to remedy the situation can be expected to understand, even if they are prepared to forget their own troubles long enough to listen and respond.

My childhood got off to a flying start but crash-landed at the age of seven. I have fond pre-school memories of ***Listen with Mother*** on the radio and great affection for my infant school days when I learned to read. I was enchanted by words and stories.

Whenever it was time to go home from school, I would put the book I was reading into my satchel to continue reading when I got home, returning it to the classroom bookshelf the next morning before selecting another. One day, to my horror, a teacher pointed an accusing finger at me as I was stuffing a partly read adventure story into my satchel and scolded, 'David, you know you don't take school books out of school!' I can still remember the disappointment I felt at being deprived of an immense pleasure.

This famine in reading material coincided with a marked deterioration in my parents' marriage and I withdrew into myself. I left both school and home in the early hours of my sixteenth birthday with no academic qualifications. The following year, I was admitted to a psychiatric hospital for ten weeks, following an attempted suicide. I did not know and would probably not have cared at the time if I had known that I was suffering from clinical (major) depression.

Anxiety, depression and mood disorders are serious problems that afflict all too many children and teenagers. Sadly, in many but not all such situations, had their parents or teachers been more informed and less preoccupied with other issues, problems could have been identified and treated—and, in some cases, prevented in the first place. What greater gift can you give a child at risk of losing their childhood, than that of restoring it?

Even if they have the most loving and caring mums and dads in the world, some children will become depressed either through biological factors, traumatic experiences, or a combination of both. Furthermore, it is a fact of life that parents cannot protect their children from all the possible causes of depression all of the time, although much pain and heartache can be avoided with early recognition and treatment when depression occurs.

In childhood, young boys are far more likely to be depressed than girls. In adolescence, however, the reverse is true. By the time children reach their teens, girls are twice as likely as boys to become depressed. It is worth noting that boys usually show different symptoms of depression from girls; when young or adolescent boys get depressed they have a tendency to become angry, disruptive, sullen, even aggressive.

The indications of depression in girls of all ages are harder to distinguish because they can be confused with behavioural patterns which are sometimes regarded as socially acceptable: withdrawal, acquiescence and passivity.

The best defence against depression that parents can give their children is to provide a stable and loving home environment and to help them to develop resilience in life. Resilient children recover more quickly from frustration, disappointment, misfortune and change. They are less likely to be overwhelmed by the challenges of childhood and adolescence and, consequently, they are far less likely to become susceptible to depression.

The most practical and enjoyable way to help very young children achieve resilience is to take an active role in their development by becoming the person they speak to, the person who interprets their experiences, who helps them to overcome their difficulties. By responding to children in this positive, revealing and encouraging way, you assist them in fashioning and shaping the foundations for a flexible coping strategy that will allow them to bounce back with ease from the ups and downs of life.

Every child is unique. The better you know your kids—their strengths and weaknesses, their likes and dislikes—the more effective you will be in helping them to develop a coping style that builds on their strengths, and not on their weaknesses. Children who are encouraged to build confidence and self-esteem on their strengths tend to become individuals who can handle stress without distress and adults who can achieve their ambitions.

In contrast, children who are frequently discouraged or placed in circumstances in which they feel overwhelmed will eventually become discouraged and overwhelmed. They may retreat into themselves in response to their feelings of helplessness and insecurity. This can and often does provide fertile ground for high anxiety, mood disorders and, ultimately, for the onset of clinical depression.

21

Depressed youngster

WHAT YOU THINK OF YOURSELF IS MUCH MORE
IMPORTANT THAN WHAT OTHERS THINK OF YOU.

—Seneca

A wise and trusted mentor is invaluable right now. Which family member, friend, confidant, school teacher or mental health professional will step up to the challenge?

Mental health problems often start in childhood, but opportunities to help are being missed here in Britain and in many countries around the world. Seventy-five per cent of mental illnesses start before a child reaches their eighteenth birthday and here is the obvious place to own up to the fact that I count myself in that statistic. My mental health problems started at the age of eleven and erupted at sixteen. As a result, my childhood was a write-off. I left school with no academic qualifications whatsoever and that was the least of my problems.

My wife is a mathematics teacher at an excellent school in Cornwall. Based on the official national statistics, in an average class of thirty students, three will have a mental health problem at any one time. The average wait for effective treatment is ten years. No, that's not a misprint. No, Britain is not a Third World country. In ten years the majority of these children will not be children.

On a typical day in school my wife will teach up to five different classes and she's just one teacher in one school. You do the maths! Are you beginning to get a grasp for the scale of the mental health problem in our schools? Nobody likes to admit to a mental health problem because it has all the wrong connotations. *But it's not your fault.* Don't be ashamed. If we want to play the blame game we could legitimately blame successive British governments for the lack of a cohesive mental health policy dating back sixty-five years. Is there any government in the world that can claim a sterling record when it comes to the nation's mental health?

The problem could so easily be solved at source in all but the most hard-core and complex cases if stress management coping strategies of the type you will encounter later in this book were taught in schools as part of the national curriculum. Students would benefit for the rest of their lives and the National Health Service could save billions of pounds over a ten year timespan. Thousands of young lives could be saved as well. Suicide is the biggest killer of young people in the United Kingdom. It is the leading cause of death in young men and women aged twenty to thirty-four.

Let's not hold our breath waiting for our respective governments to cobble together some sort of cut-price mental health policy. Self-help is the order of the day and we'll do all right. In fact, we'll do very well indeed because this is a worthwhile subject and when we get stuck into the self-therapy sessions, it'll be challenging, but fascinating and incredibly rewarding.

And to end this chapter on a promising note, parents in Britain in February 2019 have been officially told to limit their children's screen time to protect their health. For the first time ever, guidelines have been issued by the government on how long youngsters should be allowed to spend on video games, television, mobile phones and tablets.

Children should be encouraged to break off from any of the above activities at least every two hours and, most importantly, to avoid social media before bedtime, according to new guidance from chief medical officer Dame Sally Davies.

Guidance, at last! All we have to do now is to put it into practice.

22

Teen depression

WE DO NOT SEE THINGS AS THEY ARE.
WE SEE THEM AS WE ARE.

—The Talmud

Depressed teenagers need to have their feelings acknowledged and taken seriously. They need to be allowed to feel what they feel for as long as they need to feel it. They do not need to be told to snap out of it. Telling a depressed young person to grow up or not to be silly only serves to ensure that he or she will hide their true feelings in future. Nobody stays depressed if they can help it. It is the most awful, empty, joyless existence imaginable. One feels isolated and in turmoil and nothing seems to matter anymore.

Teenagers who are depressed are often unresponsive. They find it hard to tell others exactly how they feel, or what they want, and they seldom seem to have the energy to do anything constructive. One teenager, an intelligent, good-looking fifteen-year-old girl with kind, loving parents said, 'I feel so lonely, so worthless, I don't know what I want—I just want to stop all this pain.'

Typically, teenagers will fail to let their nearest and dearest know how they are feeling and what might be of help to them because they genuinely cannot see how things can improve. They may only come to know what they don't want after they have been given it, or realise what they really don't want to hear after they have been told it. Rarely, without a wise and trusted mentor,

David M Hinds

do they discover what really helps because too few of those who care about them understand.

To someone else, the fact that they feel as they do may appear unjustified, illogical or downright ungrateful, and the depressed person may well agree. But realisation alone cannot stop them feeling the way they feel because their feelings are all too real. To attempt to deny how they feel is to deny them the right to their feelings. It is tantamount to saying that your opinion in a matter that you may know little about is more valid than their feelings. It is this very same failure to accept their feelings that can contribute to depression in the first place.

Young people in their teens often assess their predicament, their prospects and their self-worth inaccurately. Based on no more evidence than a foolish, unkind or chance remark, they may come to believe that nobody will find them attractive, give them a job, invite them to the right parties, etc. It can be devastating to a teenager not to be allowed to dress and behave as their friends do and it is a supremely confident youngster who is able to resist peer-group pressure.

Bullying online, at school or college is another source of depression. Students will undoubtedly fear the bullying, but they may fear the risk of reprisals even more if they were to report it. Most survive by looking forward to the day when they will leave or by skipping classes. Those who cannot cope become depressed.

A young person whose behaviour gradually changes, who becomes either disruptive or withdrawn, needs careful assessment. There is likely to be either something seriously wrong at home, or at school, or a real or perceived problem connected with a personal relationship. In a (growing) minority of cases the problem could also be linked to drug abuse or trauma.

If your teenage children are depressed, if you truly want them to confide in you, then you must be prepared to listen but not judge. Plan the moment, seek informed advice if you need to encourage them to talk, then let them talk for as long as they want, for as long as it takes. After listening, gently probe, if appropriate, to make sure you are dealing with the real problem and that you understand it. Make your own helpful suggestions, by all means, but let them draw their own conclusions.

Your duty as a wise and trusted mentor is invaluable right now. Perhaps I have made this sound easy. It is not easy, anything but. If you are unsuited to the task, as many good people are, admit it, and seek alternative or professional help.

Simply placing a copy of this book in an appropriate place can do tremendous good should they choose to read it. You don't have to say anything, just do it. For your (or, with the consent of her parents, somebody else's) daughter, one single rose placed on top of the book will draw her attention to it. For your son—you decide!

Your role is to help them live through their depression as quickly and painlessly as possible and to tempt them out of isolation by doing everything you can think of to engage their interest, and assuage their discomfort, while accepting their feelings at face value.

23

Alone and depressed at university

I'M NOT LAZY. I'M JUST EXHAUSTED FROM FIGHTING
MY WAY THROUGH EVERY SINGLE DAY.

—Mimi Love

Download *Emoodji* and seek professional advice from your college.

University life should be a wondrous time of great learning, new friends and experiences and a greater freedom to explore new ideas and find one's true self. And for many students it is. In recent years, however, depression and anxiety have afflicted college students in Britain, America and elsewhere at ever increasing rates. Research shows that nearly twenty per cent are affected to some degree.

Why is that?

Excessive use of social media and technology are deemed to be the main offenders. An increasing number of college students are living dual virtual and real lives, and the virtual life is competing and at times becoming more important than real life. Mobile phone addiction is becoming prevalent and access to smartphone use is associated with increased sleep disturbance, depression, anxiety and overall stress levels. To most of us, the mere thought of someone waking up in the middle of the night to answer text messages would appear absurd, but to an increasing number of young people, that is the new norm.

Ask yourself: is it conducive to a good night's sleep?

Seeking out drugs is another culprit but we all know that substance abuse can only be detrimental to mental health in the end, just as smoking can only be damaging to physical health.

Don't we?

Financial stresses brought about by the rising cost of tuition fees and renting accommodation come pretty high up on the list of stressors, along with the fear of debt and worries about not getting a well-paid job after graduation.

But it's not all bad news.

On the plus side, more and more university colleges are rising to the challenge of student anxiety and depression and providing help, guidance, hotlines and hope. A really positive development by MIND, the mental health charity, is the introduction of *Emoodji*, a mobile app designed to give students a way of coping with their feelings and emotional wellbeing at university. The app provides tips on money problems, exam stress, homesickness and morale. If you're wise enough to download this simple app, then you are bound to derive tremendous benefit from the stress management therapies to come once we got the preliminaries over and done with.

24

Depression in people with learning difficulties

WORDS MAY BE FALSE AND FULL OF ART;
SIGHS ARE THE NATURAL LANGUAGE OF THE HEART.

—Thomas Shadwell, *Psyche*

'I cannot express my feelings in words. My actions may have to speak for me.'

Some people, through no fault of their own, have special difficulty in learning to talk, in looking after themselves and in coping with life in general. The problem for many people with learning difficulties is that they are not able to express their feelings easily in words. They have little option but to let their actions speak for them.

Sudden changes in behaviour or mood, withdrawal, or not being able to do things they could previously do may be signs of depression. Unfortunately, it can be all too easy for the rest of us to forget that people with learning difficulties have feelings, too.

Although depression sometimes strikes out of the blue, the departure of a favourite and trusted carer can often trigger it. Sometimes one loss can lead on to other major changes. For example, after parents have died, people with learning difficulties are often moved to emergency residential care. This means they not only lose their parents and carers, but also their homes, their familiar possessions and routines as well.

It is particularly difficult for people with learning difficulties to cope with change and this is often when depression sets in. They are usually willing to work through their feelings about unhappy events and come to terms with them, but they will need special care and assistance.

Sadly, inexperienced carers often miss the early signs of depression and a deeper depression develops. Charities like the Down's Syndrome Association in London can be of tremendous benefit at times like these. They produce a range of invaluable leaflets for carers, which have been instrumental in the preparation of advice for this chapter.

People with learning difficulties are at risk of being neglected and physically or sexually abused, because they cannot easily protect themselves, or may not be able to tell other people what has happened. Abuse may lead to depression. If you are caring for someone who is vulnerable, watch out for the warning signs that something is wrong listed on the page that follows.

Guidelines to help carers recognise depression in people with a speech impediment or learning difficulties

- Sudden or gradual changes in usual behaviour.
- Seeking assurance.
- Avoidance of one particular carer.
- Loss of familiar skills.
- Loss of bowel or bladder control.
- Loss of ability to communicate.
- Outbursts of anger, destructiveness or self-harm.
- Physical illness.
- Complaining about aches and pains.
- Wandering about aimlessly or searching for something unknown.

- The above guidelines are in addition to other common symptoms of depression which include:
- Showing little interest in activities usually enjoyed.
- Feeling tired all of the time.
- No get up and go.
- Eating too little or too much.
- Isolation.
- Difficulty in sleeping.

A number of studies have indicated that background music can be helpful in potentially stressful encounters, for instance, in circumstances when someone with learning difficulties is about to be introduced to a new carer for the first time. Similar studies have also demonstrated that soothing background music can be helpful in encouraging increased verbal communication. The indications are that music of an appropriate nature can enhance the relationship-building process and carers may wish to encourage depressed people with learning difficulties to participate in the music therapy exercise in Part Five.

25

Self-harm

A DIAGNOSIS IS BURDEN ENOUGH WITHOUT BEING
BURDENED BY SECRECY AND SHAME.

—Jane Pauley

Seek professional help at once. Self-harm is not sexy.

I sometimes wonder if there is a connection between the *Fifty Shades* trilogy and the explosion in the numbers of young people self-harming over the last decade. Maybe glamorising the notion to innocent housewives (and doubtless, their daughters) that pain can be sexy, should have come with a mental health warning?

For vulnerable young people with unresolved mental health issues, albeit anxiety, depression, self-loathing, guilt, a misguided need for self-punishment or a whole range of other rather serious problems, self-harm is not sexy. It's grotesque and downright dangerous. It can lead to death.

Think about why you would want to damage your precious body.

In some countries up to fifty per cent of people who are into self-harm—mainly young people—go on to kill themselves within a relatively short period of time by committing suicide.

Now really think it through!

Do you want to die so early in your lifespan when there are so many wonderful things for you to achieve and experience? If you're into self-harm and the statistics are applicable for the country you live in then there's a fifty-fifty chance that dead is where you'll end up pretty damn soon.

If you don't care about yourself think about your loved ones and how distraught they would be without you. If you don't care about them or you believe they don't care about you, *think about me!* I would be devastated. Apart from the sadness of your demise, just imagine the bad press I'd get. 'Vulnerable reader reads self-help book on depression that took half a lifetime of experience and expertise to write *and then…*'

I realise, of course, that you're expressing overwhelming emotional distress or trying to find a way of coping by punishing yourself or relieving unbearable tension. But is there no one that will hear your cry for help?

Who gave you this book? Does that person care? Or did you seek out this book for yourself? If so, deep down you want to survive; you want to recover and you will. You have already indicated your desire to get well by reaching out for this book. That's a fantastic start and you really should feel proud of yourself. It's not easy, I know. Cut out the self-harm because you've got the book to dig into now. Read on to the end of the book and work with me through the various exercises until you feel better about yourself, and you will. As long as you are alive and breathing, there's always hope of a better life: a better life for you.

If you live in the United Kingdom and you need someone to talk to right now, pick up the phone and dial the Samaritans 24/7 on 116123. They are lovely people and they are there for you.

In the United States of America you can call Rawhide 24/7 to talk about self-harm on 1-800-237-TALK. They genuinely want to help you and they care. Other countries may have their own special arrangements. Please refer to the Internet for up-to-date 24/7 helplines, but make sure they are legitimate before calling.

If you are desperate and incapable of cutting out the self-harm, short-circuit the system by calling 999, 911 or whatever to kick-start the process of getting yourself sorted. Wise up. Seek professional help.

To my way of thinking, there are no fifty shades of grey when it comes to self-harm, only a bleak and grey dead end. Please get off that treadmill immediately.

I would like to end this most difficult of chapters with a candid recollection of my own. Way back in my somewhat troubled youth when things were grim for me, a hard but caring individual said, "One day David, you'll look back at this period in your life and laugh."

I thought he was a mean-hearted bastard who didn't understand my pain, but in fact he did and he was right.

26

Seasonal affective disorder (SAD)

Is it so small a thing to have enjoyed the sun?
To have lived light in the spring?
To have loved, to have thought, to have done?
—Matthew Arnold, *Empedocles on Etna*

Light therapy can be effective for individuals who find their moods fluctuating with the changing seasons.

Tens of millions of people in the developed world suffer from a condition known as seasonal affective disorder (SAD). This phenomenon usually affects sufferers for approximately five months of the year. In Britain, this commences with the onset of autumn, around late October/early November, and lifts quite suddenly at the beginning of spring. Many people with SAD maintain that their feelings of depression seem to worsen the further north they live and the more overcast the prevailing weather conditions.

SAD symptoms include many of the usual symptoms of depression—decreased libido, lethargy and social withdrawal—and as the abbreviation of the disorder implies, sufferers feel sad most of the time and have little energy to get out of bed in the morning.

Many experts believe SAD to be caused by disruption to the human body clock, the circadian rhythm that co-ordinates our awareness of day (waking time) and night (sleeping time). The pineal gland inside the brain produces the hormones serotonin (the 'feel-good' substance moderated in treatment for depression by drugs such as Prozac) and melatonin (the hormone that regulates our waking and sleeping cycles and our reproductive cycle).

SAD should not be confused with the usual winter doldrums. Some people with this condition may suffer insomnia so severely that they have problems trying to maintain their efficiency at work. Additionally, a minority of sufferers may experience a craving for carbohydrates and gain considerable weight during the winter months.

Unfortunately, spending more time outside during daylight hours will not necessarily bring relief to SAD sufferers. However, light therapy has been shown to be the most effective solution for individuals who find their moods fluctuating with the changing seasons and it is widely available in specialist clinics.

Therapy consists of exposure one hour a day to a 10,000-lux light box containing a full spectrum fluorescent or incandescent light, which can be up to thirty times brighter than standard interior lighting.

Treatment is normally recommended to commence early in November and to end during the month of March, but times for treatment may vary depending on where you live. Be sure to follow the safety guidelines that your therapist will point out on your first visit.

For some SAD sufferers the condition is banished at a stroke by substituting all existing overhead light bulbs in the home with more powerful 150 watt bulbs. For safety reasons, make sure that all lampshades (which would be better removed in any event if they restrict light) can tolerate the extra heat generated by the bigger and more powerful replacement bulbs.

Finally, before concluding this chapter, I would like to touch on three further ways to help yourself get better: exercise, diet and winter breaks. The chapters on 'Getting active' and 'Food for thought' are particularly relevant to SAD sufferers with the additional recommendation that those affected should ideally exercise outside at noon (your lunch break, perhaps?) when the winter sun is brightest. It also makes sense to skip your annual summer holidays, if possible, and take winter breaks in the sun instead.

27

Depressed,
functioning on autopilot

O FOR A LIFE OF SENSATIONS RATHER THAN OF THOUGHTS!
—John Keats

Depression will lift in time. The pilot will take control. It is the experience of everyone who has suffered from depression that depressive episodes frequently vary in their intensity and these episodes may come and go for no apparent reason. The initial part of the depressive phase is usually of a reasonably slow onset, but in some more serious cases of depression, individuals can find themselves engulfed in gloom and despondency without warning.

As depression creeps up on us by stealth and silently takes us over, many of us tend to soldier on bravely with our usual way of life, denying to ourselves and to others that anything is the matter with us. We battle on as best we can, oblivious to the reality that the joy of life is gradually being squeezed out of us.

Sadness is always unpleasant but it is not as bad as depression. When we are sad, we maintain our self-respect, we feel better for a good cry, we confide in others and it helps. Not so when we are depressed: our self-respect fades and quickly deserts us and crying no longer seems to help. We feel alienated and alone because our friends and loved ones do not seem to understand how we feel and we no longer have the energy, the will, or the ability to explain.

All over the world, women have a tendency to react to depression more sensibly than men, even though a staggering fifty-seven per cent of women who suffer from pre-menstrual syndrome have thought of suicide according to a United Kingdom study of four hundred women with mild to severe PMS.

The survey was conducted for the Women's Nutritional Advisory Service (WNAS), following the sad case of sixteen-year-old schoolgirl, Ceri Kimble, who suffered so badly from PMS depression that she hanged herself at home.

More than eighty per cent of those surveyed feel violent and aggressive for up to two weeks before their periods and a disturbing ninety-two per cent feel depressed. Up to forty per cent of women suffer badly enough from PMS to consult their doctor about it and millions more may be suffering in silence. Approximately three per cent of women are forced to take up to two days off work every month because their symptoms are so severe. The WNAS claim that the best way to alleviate the symptoms of PMS is by changes in diet, nutritional supplements and an exercise and relaxation regime.

Whereas women who are suffering from a depressive illness may actively seek the company of other women for support, men tend to deny the very existence of their depression and withdraw into themselves, making matters considerably worse.

Another challenge to the medical profession is the 'smiling depressive'. This phenomenon is a variation of hypochondria whereby the individual at risk has rejected all depressive symptoms out of hand. Smiling depressives generally refer to their doctor all the aches and pains that are worrying them and then proceed to wave aside the actual diagnosis with a dismissive but valiant smile. Smiling depression is a form of masked depression and such patients often have difficulty in believing that their physical symptoms are the result of their state of mind.

In order for our condition to be classified as depression in medical terms, there needs to be clear evidence of a lowering of mood. This lowered mood may vary in intensity throughout the day but would normally prevent sufferers from being cheered up by their family or friends. This is the major distinction between being sad and suffering from depression.

When we are depressed we are largely unaffected by changing fortunes, happy events, or the efforts of those closest to us to tempt us out of isolation. Our mood does not lift in response to what happens around us. We have a tendency to remain in a state that is referred to in medical terms as 'emotionally flat and unresponsive'. Despite this invisible handicap, many of us, providing our degree of depression is not too severe, continue to work and go about our business but we are simply functioning on autopilot. We are not *living* life as it is supposed to be *lived*.

28

The 'baby blues' and postnatal depression

BABY, SLEEP A LITTLE LONGER,

TILL THE LITTLE LIMBS ARE STRONGER.

—Alfred, Lord Tennyson, *Sea Dreams*

You will survive this for your baby's sake. The 'baby blues' and post-natal depression are two very different things. Let's deal with the easy one first. After the birth of a baby almost half of all mothers suffer a period of mild depression termed 'the blues'. This may last for a few hours or a few days and then it disappears.

A mother understandably feels emotional following the birth of her baby and can cry for no apparent reason. Some mothers feel tired and lethargic, others feel anxious and tense and tend to worry a great deal. These feelings are hardly surprising because when a baby is born sudden changes take place in the mother's hormone levels. Levels of some hormones required during pregnancy drop rapidly, while others, like those needed to start the production of milk, rise. These rapid changes are believed to be responsible for triggering the blues.

Rest and quiet are most important after giving birth but few mothers get either because they are busy responding to the needs of the new baby. The support and understanding of the father is most important at this time and visitors should be encouraged not to stay too long.

Mothers who have the blues should be allowed to cry if they want to and be allowed to express their fluctuating emotions. Plenty of rest is necessary. Should they appear miserable they should not, under any circumstances, be told to 'pull yourself together' and it can be a great help to the new mum if someone will listen to her and reassure her that her worries and feelings of misery will not last and that she will soon feel better. If the blues do continue for more than a couple of days then she should see her doctor and discuss the problem.

Postnatal depression is a depressive illness that affects one in ten new mothers and it can set in during the week of the birth and up to six months afterwards. Some mothers find that they are less able than others to cope with the demands of the new baby and they may be tearful, sad and despondent, or even downright fearful. Some may even experience pain for which there is no obvious cause other than, perhaps, anxiety and tension. Many have difficulty in sleeping and have a marked reduction in appetite. It is common when suffering with postnatal depression to lose interest in sex. This symptom can last for some time and it is helpful if one's partner can be patient and accept that normal sexual desire will return as soon as depression lifts.

Many women find that their depression becomes worse just before, or during, a period. An effective solution can be to ask your doctor to consider progesterone therapy to help prevent this severe form of pre-menstrual tension. At difficult times like these it is essential to maintain a healthy diet and vitamin B6 or a general vitamin supplement may be advisable.

Obviously, I have no first-hand experience of postnatal depression to offer you. However, the beautiful Iranian wife of one of my best friends, a nice guy from America, suffered from postnatal depression in a bad way. I remember visiting her at the height of her depression and being taken aback by the depth of her suffering. She is now completely well and a very fine mother to her son.

There is also a very rare form of postnatal depression called postpartum psychosis. Only about one in one thousand mothers will suffer from this and it requires immediate medical treatment. Symptoms include hallucinations, delusions, suicidal thoughts and attempts to harm the baby. Tragically, in exceptional cases of post-partum psychosis, which have gone undiagnosed, mothers have killed their new-born babies and/or themselves.

The most important thing you can do to help yourself if you are a mother suffering from depression is to believe that you can and will get better. Depression, however frightening, is never permanent. There are organisations and self-help groups throughout the world to help you through this difficult time.

It's also worth bearing in mind that breastfeeding may protect mothers against depression in later life. An international study conducted jointly in the USA and South Korea found that women who fed their babies naturally were almost two thirds less likely to suffer from mental health problems. And the more children they had, the greater the positive effect.

This important study, published in January 2019 in the Journal of Affective Disorders, looked at more than one thousand two hundred mothers now in their fifties and older, who had gone through the menopause.

The lead author of the report, Dr Sangshin Park of Brown University in Providence, Rhode Island, said, "Our study findings indicate that breastfeeding is beneficial, not only to infants' short-term and long-term health, but also to maternal psychological health."

The World Health Organisation recommends exclusively breastfeeding during the first six months of the baby's life, but less than one third of British mothers try breastfeeding at all.

29

'I'm a man: we don't "do" depression'

—TELLING ONE'S SORROWS OFTEN BRINGS COMFORT.

Pierre Corneille, *Polyeucte*

Fact—men find it difficult to admit to psychological problems.

Depression is an illness that affects both men and women, but GPs throughout the world report treating far fewer men than women for depression. It seems likely that men suffer from depression just as much as women but because of their 'macho' mentality they are less likely to admit to depression or to ask for help.

Come on, guys, the game is up! We suffer every bit as much as those lovely ladies but because they are reputed to be the gentler sex, they feel able to put their tender hands up to depression, while we bury our heads in the pillow and suffer in agonising silence.

It is the way we often think about ourselves in matters of mental health that can be unhelpful. Compared with women, we have a tendency to be far more concerned with being competitive, powerful and successful. Most of us simply cannot admit that we can be fragile or extremely vulnerable. Traditionally, we have been conditioned to think that as males we should depend on ourselves and that it is weak to have to depend on someone else—a doctor, for instance—even for a short time.

To compound matters further, this traditionally tough and self- reliant view of how men should be is held by some women.

Men can find that owning up to their weaknesses can result in their partner rejecting them.

Men, unless they have been specially trained, do not have the ability to cope with disagreements and upsets as well as women do. Arguments have a tendency to make men feel physically uncomfortable and they will usually try to avoid all manner of difficult discussions by making excuses or going out for a drink. Furthermore, men have traditionally seen themselves as the breadwinners and leaders of their families, but are finding that it is women who most often start the process of separation and divorce.

According to the Royal College of Psychiatrists in Great Britain in their admirable booklet entitled *Men Behaving Sadly,* men are around three times more likely than women to kill themselves. Suicide is most common among men who are separated, widowed or divorced and is more likely in someone who is a heavy drinker. We do know that two out of three men who kill themselves have seen their GP in the previous four weeks and nearly half of them have seen their doctor in the week directly before they kill themselves.

Men who are depressed are more likely to talk about the physical symptoms of their depression rather than the emotional and psychological ones. This may be one reason why doctors sometimes fail to diagnose depression in men. If you are feeling wretched, even suicidal, don't hold back—tell your GP exactly how you feel and then they can help you. Try to remember that depression is a result of chemical changes that take place in the brain. It is nothing to do with being weak or unmanly.

Many men who recover from depression, including me, emerge stronger and better able to cope than before. You may see situations and relationships more clearly in the future and find the strength and the wisdom to make important decisions and changes that perhaps you were avoiding before.

30

Depressed in retirement

I LOVE EVERYTHING THAT'S OLD: OLD FRIENDS,
OLD TIMES, OLD MANNERS, OLD BOOKS, OLD WINES.
—Oliver Goldsmith, *She Stoops to Conquer*

It is better to wear out than to rust out.

Retirement can pose a tremendous problem for people who relied upon their job to give them purpose and structure in life. Except for those people who relish the prospect of retirement and have many other interests or projects in mind, retirement, when it comes, can seem bleak and unstructured. Many retirees miss going to work, they miss their workmates and they find themselves wondering how everybody is coping without them. Sooner or later, they are forced to conclude that their former colleagues are probably managing perfectly well without them, and that realisation brings with it a certain emptiness: a chilling awareness of being destined for the scrap heap.

According to a MORI poll commissioned by the UK charity, Help the Aged, in association with British Gas and conducted nationwide, older people in Britain are facing an epidemic of loneliness and isolation. More than a million of those over sixty-five revealed that they felt trapped in their own homes. Even more disturbing is the revelation that no fewer than eighteen per cent of them say they have gone *for a whole week* without speaking to friends, neighbours or family.

Mervyn Kohler, head of policy at Help the Aged, said, 'This survey graphically illustrates the sheer scale of the terrible loneliness and isolation felt by many older people in Britain.'

You shouldn't feel lonely, isolated or depressed just because you are old. If you feel this way, don't hesitate: contact your doctor, your Social Services Department, or the local or regional office of Help the Aged, and ask for help. Despite evidence to the contrary, this is still a caring country and there is someone sitting behind a desk right now (or there will be at 9 a.m.) waiting to help you. With the best will in the world, they can't tell you about the wonderful initiatives and opportunities available to you to meet socially with others unless they are made aware of your predicament.

In my experience of working with the older generation as a stress management consultant, they are a wily lot; they have known tough times before! Once they have been given sound advice and pointed in the direction of a solution, they can often steal a march on their younger counterparts because they have recourse to a lifetime of wisdom and experience.

Do make the effort to get out whenever you can. I know it can be difficult when you are old because of physical problems like stiff joints or swollen ankles, but it is worthwhile. Staying at home all the time can make you brood on things. This really doesn't help and actually makes you feel more helpless and depressed. So, whenever neighbours, family, friends, charity workers or the local community warden offer assistance, let them help you to get out. Even if you are not interested in making new friends, it is a good idea to have some diversity and excitement in your life to keep boredom at bay. If you go to a day centre, they may have their own transport that you can use. Above all, be open to new possibilities.

My aunt Freda, crippled at birth and born with no neck, has lived alone in north London ever since the death of my grandmother. I am not aware that she has ever had a partner—not until a few years ago that is, at the age of seventy-nine—when a retired

British Army captain stopped her in the street and offered to carry her bag of shopping for her.

Instead of instinctively saying, 'No, thank you', she studied him, smiled her lovely smile and said, 'Yes, please.' This simple act of chivalry marked the beginning of the most wonderful period in her life until, sadly, last year, Robert died. My aunt, for the first time in her life, had discovered the joy of love and her life is richer and more meaningful for the experience. She has fond and happy memories of their short time together that sustained her until her own death.

So, the recipe for a happy retirement is to gently bring to a close your previous working life (unless you can benefit from it from home, of course), be open to new possibilities and move on. This doesn't mean you can't remember your achievements with pride and enjoy thinking and talking about the old times. It just means you should avoid being frozen into your former working life.

David M Hinds

31

Depression in terminal illness

DIE, MY DEAR DOCTOR? THAT'S THE LAST THING I SHALL DO.
—Lord Palmerston

Some terminal patients defy their doctor's prognosis and refuse to die as predicted: *they get better!*

Why do some patients recover from critical conditions when their doctors believe there is no hope of recovery? What do survivors do that makes the difference between life and death?

Bernie Siegel, the American physician and author of the book, *Love, Medicine and Miracles*, observed that many patients who were ultimately successful in recovering from advanced stages of cancer had been described by doctors and nursing staff as 'difficult patients'. He says that whenever he consults on a case he is encouraged to see in a patient's medical notes entries such as: 'uncooperative', 'questions why tests are ordered', 'demands to be informed about test results' and 'insists on explanations about treatments'.

Siegel, as a result of his work with cancer patients, is convinced that terminal patients who get better instead of dying react to their prognosis as a 'wake-up call' to their very existence. They make far-reaching changes in how they think, act, talk and feel: reforming their eating and social habits and spending every waking hour masterminding their own recovery.

Siegel believes there are three categories of terminal patients: he estimates that around 15 to 20 per cent at some level of consciousness wish to die and will probably do so no matter how excellent their treatment. About 60 to 70 per cent passively co-operate with their doctors in every respect and will do whatever they are told to do, including dying when predicted if that is the doctor's prognosis. Around 15 to 20 per cent are exceptional patients. They reject the probability of becoming a statistic and refuse to be discouraged by the odds against survival.

On the day of the UK launch of my first health book, *After Stroke,* I appeared on the ITV network programme *This Morning* with Richard and Judy. In the live television phone-in that followed our discussion on the book and serious illness, a woman who had been told by doctors seven years previously that she had a life expectancy of two weeks due to cancer which had been deemed inoperable, phoned in to tell us that she was very much alive and kicking.

The show's joint host, Richard Madeley, in his own inimitable style, asked her, 'Why are you not dead? How come the "Grim Reaper" didn't get you?'

It transpired that her story had a lot in common with the views of many leading doctors and psychologists: survivors are not easy patients. She had been defiant, angry, indignant and not at all ready to die. By her own admission, she was not an easy patient and refused to accept the prognosis of imminent death. She used her anger (which sets off the stress hormones adrenalin, noradrenalin and cortisol, arousing tension in the body) to fuel her desperate quest to find a way, *any way*, of cheating death. She resorted to praying, healthy eating, positive thinking and self-talk (convincing her mind, body and soul that she really was defeating her cancer), plus just about anything else that she could think of. Even the most sceptical of readers must concede that something must have worked because she is still here with us now, fit and well and cancer-free.

In essence, she showed herself to be willing to adopt and utilise any possible action or reaction to aid her recovery. She expected to be able to influence events concerning her own body in a way that would lead to a satisfactory outcome and she was proved right.

I can relate to her recovery. In 1995, after two strokes and a subclavian bypass operation, I remember staring up at the ceiling from my hospital bed, partly paralysed and unable to comprehend the words of a newspaper, thinking: 'Is this me?... Yes it is, but I'll be back!'

I promised myself there and then that I would reclaim every single one of my faculties and then write a book based on my experiences. It took me many years but I made good on all aspects of that promise. Sir Peter Morris, Nuffield Professor of Surgery at the University of Oxford, carried out my operation and was generous enough to write a foreword to the book, in which he quoted an entry made in my medical records by nursing staff: 'He is extremely angry about his condition and shows this in his relationships with his carers.'

These difficult patients question why alternative treatments are not being offered and may insist that their doctor try something different. They are patients with 'an attitude' fuelled by the unshakeable will to get well. They hold the view that although they need the expertise and care of their doctor, they are very much in charge of themselves and this is not necessarily an attitude that all doctors fully understand or are equipped to deal with.

At this point, we need to make an important distinction between the terminally ill and the seriously ill patient. The information in this chapter is intended primarily for the terminally ill patient who may feel defeated and depressed but who really wants to live. The advice I would offer to any seriously ill, but not terminally ill, patient, would be very different: I would stress the need to relax, keep calm and to take things easy; co-operating fully with the medical team in order to secure the best possible recovery available to them.

There are tens of thousands of people alive and kicking and enjoying their lives today who were not expected to live or to make a one hundred per cent recovery. Because of limited space in this chapter, you have read about only two. If, despite all, you still possess the will to live, why not give recovery all you have got and then some? It seems to me that you have everything to gain and nothing to lose. Don't worry about being a less than perfect patient: doctors and nursing staff harbour a secret admiration for survivors and so do I.

Is it possible for doctors to be right on every occasion when they predict life or death? Sometimes the terminally ill patient survives! Can you steel yourself to believe that the doctor could be wrong in your case and fight to live?

32

Clinical depression

IN THE REAL DARK NIGHT OF THE SOUL IT
IS ALWAYS THREE O'CLOCK IN THE MORNING.
—F. Scott Fitzgerald, *The Crack-Up*

Depression, although frightening, is never permanent. Clinical depression is a disorder requiring intervention and treatment, just as any physical illness would require attention. Clinical depression, which is often referred to as major depression, a mood disorder or an affective disorder, is one of the most incapacitating of all chronic conditions in terms of social functioning.

It ranks second only to heart disease in exacting a physical toll, measured by days in bed and feelings of general discomfort. It is more disabling than many of the major chronic organic disorders, and its economic cost, in terms of lost working time and poor performance, is enormous.

Clinical depression adversely affects our thought patterns and mood, our feelings, our energy levels and our overall ability to function normally, as well as our physical wellbeing. It is most certainly not just a matter of feeling 'blue' or 'under the weather'. It's more intense than feeling sad or experiencing grief following the loss of a loved one and, most serious of all, there is a high incidence of suicide amongst the clinically depressed.

I would not wish the pain and isolation of clinical depression on my worst enemy, but if you are unfortunate enough to be suffering from this devastating illness right now, you will ultimately have an opportunity to get everything right in your life for the future.

As human beings, we learn very little from good fortune, power, prosperity and the easy life. The real lessons in life are learned through trial and misfortune, rather as you are experiencing now.

I learned the hard way, too, and although this may come as something of a shock to you in your present condition, I am grateful for the lesson—gruelling as it was at the time.

Now, instead of missed opportunities, broken romances, and shallow living, I have an enviable and sustainable lifestyle doing what I enjoy doing—writing! I live where I live because, generally speaking, Devon and Cornwall folk are pleasant and I am not willing to move away to more exotic places. Despite my failings, ill health and mistakes of the past, I have found happiness and contentment.

Why am I telling you all this when you are feeling so miserable? Am I a sadist? I want you to know that the reason is because the seeds of my happiness were sown in the misery of serious illness. My distress was so great that I decided to do whatever it took to get better and stay that way. Now you have the essential tools you will need to do the same, laid out in a book for you. Read this book carefully. I wrote it for you.

Later, when we have dealt with the mundane but necessary aspects of your illness and you are beginning to feel a little better, I will show you how to reach for your finest hour and put real meaning into your life.

The key to release from all that pain you have been suffering may be staring you in the face, or be inside your heart, or you may have to look in a completely different direction. Propelled by your eagerness not to feel as you have of late, very soon you will have the momentum to achieve the seemingly impossible and I will show you how to use that special brand of energy for your own personal benefit.

Clinical depression is a tragedy by any standards, but much good can come out of it if we are persuaded to put right what is wrong in our lives. Some people may see it as a signpost, a forced opportunity to do something else, something meaningful, with their lives. Right now, the only sensible thing you can do is to remain calm and focused on beating depression. In the closing chapters of the book, when you have absorbed all those things that you must absorb in order to be free of depression for life, your heart will begin to pound with excitement as we touch upon some of the distinct possibilities for happiness for you.

33

Depression requiring specialist intervention

I DO NOT KNOW WHETHER I WAS THEN A MAN
DREAMING I WAS A BUTTERFLY, OR WHETHER I AM NOW
A BUTTERFLY DREAMING I AM A MAN.

—Chuang-Tzu

The term 'clinical depression' is used to categorise any form of depression where symptoms are severe and lasting enough to require treatment. The general advice and guidance in this book is believed to be suitable for those suffering from any depressive disorder, however mild or severe the symptoms. There are, however, some forms of depression that exceed the scope of this book and those afflicted will require specialist medical intervention. Brief descriptions of these conditions follow:

Melancholic depression is a severe form of clinical depression in which the patient has lost virtually all interest in the activities of life and does not respond positively—even temporarily—when something good happens. Quite simply, the patient has lost the ability to experience pleasure. By contrast, most people with severe clinical depression can usually be cheered up by good news—albeit temporarily.

Manic-depressive psychosis is a condition that takes the form of alternating periods of extreme melancholia and equally extreme periods of elation and excitement. A more technical term used to describe some patients who typify many aspects of this diverse and complex category is 'bi-polar affective disorder'.

The manic element of the disorder is an abnormal exaggeration of the feelings of elation and excitement that we all experience from time to time. Some notable writers, artists and composers are believed to have suffered from this condition, including Ernest Hemingway, Charles Dickens, Virginia Woolf, Mark Twain, Beethoven, Van Gogh and Mahler.

When someone is experiencing a manic episode for the first time, the person concerned may not realise that there is anything abnormal in his or her behaviour. It is often a family member, a friend or colleague, who is the first to notice that something is not quite right.

Atypical depression, which usually starts in adolescence and can be persistent rather than periodic, turns the typical symptoms of depression upside down. While people with most types of depression have a tendency to sleep and eat less than normal, patients with this kind of depression tend to oversleep, over-eat and gain weight rapidly. They can be very sensitive to rejection, particularly romantic rejection.

Schizophrenia is a serious mental illness that affects one per cent of the global population. There is abundant scientific evidence (though as yet no conclusive proof) to suggest that faulty genes may contribute to the onset of the illness. The illness generally becomes apparent in the sufferer's late teens or early twenties—although it can be middle age or even later before symptoms become apparent. Patients are usually advised, because of the risk of repeated episodes, to continue taking medication for many years, perhaps for the rest of their lives.

Sadly, schizophrenia causes tremendous difficulty and distress for the afflicted and their families. Not only do sufferers have to contend with the likelihood of hallucinations, delusions and interruptions to their train of thought, they also have to live with the image of a deranged killer as portrayed in so many films and TV programmes—a representation which is far from typical.

One point concerning depression of any type should be noted above all others. No less an authority than the *Oxford Companion to the Mind,* advises, 'All persons suffering from depression should be adequately assessed for the risk of suicide. Relatives, and some physicians, sometimes hesitate to enquire directly about suicidal thoughts lest such questions prompt the actions they are most anxious to prevent.'

The evidence is that most depressed patients answer truthfully to enquiries of this kind and may even be relieved by the opportunity to discuss their innermost feelings of despair and dread of the future.

34

Suicidal tendencies

MY FORTUNE SOMEWHAT RESEMBLED THAT OF A PERSON
WHO SHOULD ENTERTAIN AN IDEA OF COMMITTING SUICIDE,
AND, ALTOGETHER BEYOND HIS HOPES, MEET
WITH THE GOOD HAP TO BE MURDERED.
—Nathaniel Hawthorne, *The Custom House*

We only die once; and it's for such a long, long time…

I attempted suicide in my teens. I was led to believe that I was not an easy child and I should imagine there is much truth in that. My father suffered from depression and my grandfather, so I was told, had been depressed for much of his life. My uncle had attempted suicide early in life. Sadly, his only son did commit suicide early in life and my uncle has been devastated ever since.

I left home, school and London aged sixteen, following major disagreements at home. I didn't bother to take any exams or complete the academic year. On reflection, one or two of the teachers at my school, particularly my mathematics teacher, were supportive and tried to help me. I think they suspected there had been something the matter with me for years, but I could not bring myself to communicate with anyone beyond a certain no-go level.

I moved to Liverpool, working in a camera shop in the city centre and living across the Mersey on the Wirral in a youth hostel. For a reason that might seem inconsequential and incomprehensibly minor to anyone not consumed by depression, I decided to kill myself because I didn't have enough money to pay the rent.

I went to the doctor and extracted a prescription for sleeping pills from him. He was most sympathetic and reached for his pen without too much hesitation when I told him that I hadn't been able to sleep ever since my sister had been killed in a car crash (she hadn't).

On my way back from the chemist, I went in to a sweet shop and spent the remainder of my money on a giant-size packet of liquorice allsorts which I consumed with relish—particularly the round pink and yellow coconut ones with liquorice in the middle—along with the entire pack of sleeping pills. There was no suicide note. I had nothing to say to anyone. I had no regrets, no second thoughts, and soon afterwards, no thoughts at all.

The next thing I knew, there was a group of doctors and nurses around me. 'Can you see us? Can you see us? Can you see anything at all?'

The reason for their concern became apparent when I had recovered sufficiently to look at myself in a mirror. My eyes were nowhere to be seen. All that was visible when they were open were two slits where my eyes used to be.

Adults and children who commit suicide are typically those who feel that death is the only way of escaping from what seems to them an impossible life without hope, although, in some cases, it is a threat or a cry for help that went unheeded. The decision to commit suicide and the actions taken towards that intention are invariably the consequences of negative thinking—the primary characteristic of depression.

Suicide is still rare in children under the age of twelve. However, the rate of suicide among teenagers has trebled in the last thirty years. Suicide has now become the second highest cause of death among older teenagers in England, the United States and Sweden. The risk of actual suicide in the year following a previous attempt is nearly one hundred times greater than that in the general population.

Way back in January 2019, British Health Secretary Matt Hancock ordered web giants to crack down on suicide and self-harm images online or face new laws to stop vulnerable children being bombarded with horrific material. More people commit suicide today than die in road accidents. This cannot go on.

On March 27th 2021, the Department of Health and Social Care in the UK announced a £500 million mental health action plan to support hundreds of thousands of adults and children with mental health issues. In 2022, the World Health Organization (WHO) launched their all-important World Mental Health Report titled Transforming mental health for all. Help and support should become available for us all. But each of us must embrace the skills necessary to cope with life in the modern world.

We can start now.

By 'we' I mean you and me. It is easier for me these days: I have learned to stop the negative thoughts that feed depression at source.

With your help, I can show you how to do the same. Read on, the good bits are yet to come.

PART FOUR

Means of Recovery

35

Neuroscience to the rescue

ANY MAN COULD, IF HE WERE SO INCLINED, BE
THE SCULPTOR OF HIS OWN BRAIN.

—Santiago Ramón y Cajal

This is the beginning of the end of your depression.

In case you are wondering who this Santiago bloke I have quoted above is, and are perhaps thinking, *'How dare he make such a bold statement?'* allow me to introduce him? He is a famous scientist, often referred to as the father of neuroscience. Santiago Ramón y Cajal was the joint Noble prize winner in physiology or medicine in 1906 in recognition of work on the structure of the nervous system.

He was not kidding when he inferred that anyone could sculpture their own brain. We have all been doing it in one way or another, sometimes haphazardly, since we were born. And now you, in order to access the coping skills to beat depression, are about to learn how to sculpture your brain so that you are free to enjoy life and make the best of opportunities that come your way. You do not need to be intelligent or gifted in order to be able to achieve this apparent miracle.

You will beat depression by using the power of thought and imagination to change your entrenched outlook, teamed with a few little assignments so that you master everything thoroughly and get lots of practice. But it will be fun, beneficial and so rewarding. You get your mental health back and you learn new coping skills that are yours for ever. You may even end up happier and more contented than you have ever been in your life so far.

I know I am, and I know how and why.

During my struggle to recover from a severe stroke that half-paralysed me and sent me spiralling to the depths of depression, I used my expertise as a stress management consultant to fine-tune Santiago's brain sculpturing techniques in order to make my own recovery happen. That learning experience changed me as a person for the better. After two failed marriages and a long period of living alone, I married again. And guess what. This, my third and final marriage, turned out to be a winner. Against all odds, eighteen years into the marriage, we're both supremely happy. But we would never have got together in the first place if I hadn't learned to open my heart and share my emotions.

How could this possibly be?

I had to refashion my brain (or sculpture it as Santiago puts it) in order to recover from stroke and depression. And as I go through life now in old age, I marvel at the many other benefits of the refashioning job that I would never have got around to had it not been for my illness.

Incidentally, the refashioning bit is actually quite simple; anyone with basic ability can do it. It turns out that the brain, all one hundred billion neurons of it, the most complex entity known to man, responds to sculpturing or refashioning according to straightforward instructions. All that is required is a whole lot of focused attention and dedicated practice. Everything you need to know to succeed in this task I will explain in easily digestible, bite-size chunks throughout the rest of the book.

Rest assured this is not some sort of vague new-age concept; this is an actual physical phenomenon, measurable by brain scanning technology with the different pathways visible on a screen. From learning to change behaviour and control emotions in a different way, the core of change simply involves sculpturing/ refashioning the brain. Fortunately, this process does not need to be fully understood to benefit from its power, which allows me to cover everything you need to know to beat depression without getting complicated.

Actors do it. Athletes do it. Musicians do it. Formula One racing car drivers do it. Just about every top-class motivational speaker recommends doing it. What is the phenomenon that gives professionals the winning edge and also provides every man woman and child with an escape route from depression?

Imagination!

Mental practice, used alternatively with actual practice, is an effective tool for recovery from depression. It also has the distinct advantage of being free, easy, absolutely safe, and it can be practised just about anywhere. Back to Santiago and his sculpturing of the brain, or refashioning of the brain as I like to put it. While you're having fun and games imagining and practising better outcomes for your thoughts, your actions, and your life in general, the sculpturing or refashioning of your brain is actually taking place, the miracle of neuroscience is working in your favour. With the new, more positive mindset you will be developing, the haze of depression will simply lift like a disappearing fog.

But first we have a few odd jobs to do to clear the way for progress...

36

Dumping excess baggage

HOW MANY THINGS I CAN DO WITHOUT!

—Socrates

You can learn to let go of your bitter memories, your prejudices and your bad habits.

To bring about complete and lasting recovery from depression, you will need the freedom to open up new lines of communication between your mind, body and spirit. This will prove to be an exciting learning curve.

Before we can realistically move forward out of depression and stay that way, most of us have some excess baggage to dump. The baggage I am referring to is personal, very personal indeed: those aspects of an individual's character that manifest themselves as bad habits, prejudices, self-destructive thoughts and patterns of behaviour. These are personal liabilities we can live without and they may well have been a contributing factor in the onset of depression in the first place.

How did we acquire these and what must we do to dump them?

For the answer we invariably have to look back to our formative years. The foundation of almost every non-hereditary characteristic we possess, good and bad, stems from our childhood conditioning. Our parents and guardians start out with the best of intentions, of course, but few of them are experts in the art of raising children and many of them make mistakes, the ramifications of which may be felt by their offspring for a lifetime. Unless, later in life, one decides to put matters right once and for all—and that is where you are now.

Never mind that you are not to blame—be magnanimous—take the responsibility upon yourself to do what needs to be done. The challenge to become yourself will be hugely rewarding and worth every effort.

In future chapters, I will advise you how to go about the dumping, which is a multifaceted procedure. When you have read these chapters you will experience a supremely uplifting sensation of release from inner complication and baggage. You will find yourself free at last to allow easy flowing lines of communication between your mind, body and spirit. Real progress will be there for all to see just as soon as you start to make the little changes, one after another, that are suggested in the chapters to come. You will have commenced the process of reconnecting your disconnected self and, as a direct and predictable consequence of your actions, depression will lift.

37

Thought-stopping strategies

LIFE DOES NOT CONSIST MAINLY—OR EVEN LARGELY—OF
FACTS AND HAPPENINGS. IT CONSISTS MAINLY OF THE STORM OF
THOUGHTS THAT ARE FOREVER BLOWING THROUGH ONE'S MIND.
—Mark Twain

Empty your mind for one beautiful moment.

We are about to discover, in this short chapter, how to begin to stop, at will, the storm of thoughts that are forever blowing through our minds. This will allow us to interrupt, minimise and eventually eliminate, all those anxiety-producing, depressing and self-defeating thoughts which plague us so much of the time.

The procedures for doing this are enjoyable and straightforward. We shall call the process 'SOS' because this is an internationally recognised distress code that you are unlikely to forget and it just happens to be an abbreviation for the experiences I want you to enjoy: silence, oblivion and serenity.

To achieve a high measure of success in SOS, you will need to set aside ten minutes a day for thirty consecutive days to practise immersing your mind into this tranquil but, at the same time, disciplined state, which is not unlike meditation. The dividends you will get for this small investment in time are immeasurable. Your recovery will be greatly accelerated and you will continue to enjoy the therapeutic benefits of SOS for the rest of your life.

Press on with your practice sessions, even if you are one of those people (like me) who find new techniques a little tricky to understand at the outset. This is like escaping to an internal paradise for a few enchanted moments and discovering, on your return, that a curative lotion has been applied to your troubled mind. It is too good to give up just because you may not be able to get it right the first few times you try.

The type of thoughts we are going to target and stop are the unwanted, repetitive, sometimes irrational and frequently obsessive ones that invade our minds when we should be considering more important matters, or enjoying our leisure time.

The things you will need to prepare for your first SOS experience, which, ideally, should commence today or tomorrow, are: a lighted candle, a quiet, darkened room or a safe, peaceful hideaway, and the freedom of mind that comes with knowing that you will not be disturbed by anyone, or anything, during your ten-minute session. No ticking clocks, mobile phones, or other potential distractions.

The object of the first session is to empty your mind for one beautiful moment of all thoughts, to stop thinking, to experience nothingness. If this sounds too easy, just wait until you try! To begin with, it might seem almost impossible to silence all those irritating little thoughts for a mere two seconds, let alone ten or twenty, but with persistence and regular sessions of SOS you will succeed in emptying your mind for several minutes at a time. By then, you will be primed for the first of many bonuses to come in future chapters: you will be ready to absorb techniques that will allow you to use more of your mind than usual; you will be in a position to empower yourself to beat depression.

In order to get started, place the lighted candle on a table or on a stable surface in front of where you are going to sit, make yourself comfortable, close your eyes and concentrate on the flickering of the flame in the darkness. Even with your eyes closed you will still be aware of the flame. For as long as possible, think of nothing; do not entertain any thoughts of any kind in your mind at all. If a thought enters your head, blink, flick it out, and start again.

Roughly five to ten minutes of SOS a day, for thirty days, that's all I ask. You have no idea how much benefit you stand to gain from this part of the exercise, and the multiple gains to come when we are in a position to put together all the pieces of the puzzle.

David M Hinds

38

Using your mind to beat depression

LET US TRAIN OUR MINDS TO DESIRE
WHAT THE SITUATION DEMANDS.

—Seneca

Master this concept and life gets easier.

The situation demands that we train our minds to beat depression and that is what we shall do. In this part of the book we are going to train our minds to neutralise anger, tame fear, get active, sleep well, practise positive imagery, increase self-esteem and learn to forgive.

To make solid progress in the remaining chapters of this section, I must ask you to participate in the mind exercises and other mini-assignments I shall give you, regardless of any initial misgivings or scepticism you may have. Put all doubts on hold for a while, defer judgement, at least until you reach the end of Part Four.

The tool we are going to use to derive maximum benefit from the challenges ahead is revised thinking, a subject that we touched on earlier. Thoughts are all-powerful and it is our own thoughts that play a major role in making us depressed (or otherwise) and in keeping us depressed. All the spectacular creations of humanity (such as the Taj Mahal or the *Mona Lisa*) and the less spectacular ones (such as the Milton Keynes Shopping Centre or the Millennium Dome) began as mere thoughts. From the thought came the idea, from the idea came the plan, and from the plan the real thing evolved.

Your feelings of depression first came into being as thought. This book started as one, simple thought. I liked the idea and took it forward. If my second thought had been 'No, I can't or won't do it', you wouldn't be reading this now. Likewise, if you allow yourself to think, 'I can't' or 'I won't participate in these silly mind exercises', you slam the door on recovery.

Understandably, when we are depressed, we can make the mistake of assuming that our feelings are at fault, when the real problem is probably the way we are thinking about life in general. Many of us have a tendency to blame ourselves for everyday events that happen and to put the worst possible interpretation on things that are said to us.

This misguided and rather selective way of thinking is self-defeating and further fuels our feelings of low self-esteem and depression. To recover from depression quickly and to overcome all obstacles in the path of your recovery, you will need to adopt a new way of thinking, one which is forward-looking and blame-free. In the chapters to come you will learn how to differentiate between outmoded thinking and revised thinking.

Approach these chapters with an open mind and a willingness to experiment with the exercises and ideas suggested and very soon you could be amazed at your progress. If you haven't already scheduled time for your first session of SOS (silence, oblivion and serenity) as suggested in the previous chapter, do it now. It is an important preparatory step in preparing your mind for what you are about to accomplish.

David M Hinds

39

Neutralising anger

A SOFT ANSWER TURNETH AWAY WRATH:
BUT GRIEVOUS WORDS STIR UP ANGER.
—The Bible, Proverbs 15:1

Anger is a logical reaction to many real-life situations and confirmation that we are responding in an alert manner to an undesirable state of affairs. However, the way in which we handle our anger in response to provocation, frustration or bad news determines whether the outcome will be the best available in the circumstances, or potentially depression-inducing.

Before we learn how to neutralise our own anger, let's first observe how some people mismanage their anger and succeed primarily in damaging themselves: listen to people arguing, and you will hear the determination of each party to hold on to their 'little bit of truth', to defend it as if their life depended on it. Such limiting assumptions carry a heavy price in terms of pain, conflict and anxiety. Convincing yourself that you must be right (in contrast to other people deciding you are right) is the great booby prize in life, the one unhappy people settle for.

At one time or another, most of us find ourselves involved in situations which can give rise to anger. Sometimes, however, it is unwise, irrational or inappropriate to express those feelings directly. For instance, many of us have found ourselves in circumstances where we've known that expressing our anger will get us nowhere.

This may happen even when we are careful to express ourselves in a reasonable and non-threatening manner, but it usually happens when we have been insensitive to somebody else's feelings, at a difficult time of the month, or after one drink too many.

We are all angry people—some of us just show it more than others. Anger is usually triggered by an event, an unkind remark, a person's behaviour towards us or our interpretation of any one of those things. It sets off our stress hormones, adrenalin, noradrenalin and cortisol, arousing tension in the body.

Holding on to anger is dangerous to health. Suppressed or internalised anger can lead to high blood pressure and can make depression even worse. If something or someone has made you angry, or if you have made someone else angry and you regret your actions, rectify the situation with the person concerned at the earliest opportunity, offering a sincere apology, if appropriate.

If it is just not practical or possible to do this, release those feelings of anger and frustration in the privacy of your home, or some other safe haven. Suggestions to help you accomplish this are included in the following five exercises.

Act out your anger

Once you are alone at home, or somewhere that you consider to be a safe environment, put on some lively music, turn up the volume, and immerse yourself in the sound and the beat of the music. Allow yourself to work out and release your feelings of anger and frustration by dancing and singing along with the music, cursing, swearing, jumping, shouting or screaming at will, until you have exhausted and purged yourself of all harmful energies.

Breathe and believe in the power of words

Turn off the radio, TV and any music that may be on, sit down, take off your shoes, relax and take three slow, deep breaths, and say the words, 'I am becoming calm, I am becoming more and more calm, I am calm', until it is true. Now link the source of your anger with the culprit in a dismissive and non-confrontational manner. For instance, if you work in a pub, restaurant or shop and a regular customer has angered you, tell yourself something like, 'This guy is a real pain, but we need his money and I love this job. He means nothing to me personally and I refuse to give him another thought', or 'Now that I am relaxed and calm, I will work out a strategy so that this won't happen again.'

The letter from hell!

Now it's your turn to have some fun and derive some real benefit from your anger at the expense of the perpetrator of your emotional turmoil. While it can be tremendously therapeutic to act out your anger as suggested in the first example, or to stare it out as in our next exercise, the person who most needs to hear and understand your pain is you. Letting the offender have it in the form of a 'no holds barred' letter can release your anger and make emotional resolution easier to achieve. Allow yourself the freedom of writing a letter of protest and pour out all your pent-up emotions and negative feelings on to the page. Spare the offender nothing. Do not censor your letter in any way. Be careful! Do not mail this letter. It is exclusively for your therapeutic benefit. When you have finished it, destroy it.

The healing mirror

Another way of dealing with anger is to confront it head on in the mirror. Don't be tempted to shy away from your image just because your angry self looks so distressed. Hold your nerve and continue to look. You will very quickly feel the urge to calm down if only because you look ridiculous when fuming and angry. At this point in the exercise you may find tears welling up in your eyes. That's good. Very good. Already venom and anger are bailing out through the windows!

Imagination to the rescue

This final suggestion is my personal favourite. When you have wronged someone and tried your level best to put things right, but the person concerned just won't accept your apology, or when you believe you have been wronged, but know you haven't a cat in hell's chance of being offered an apology, use your imagination. Imagine that your apology has now been accepted on the understanding that you learn from this episode and do not repeat your mistake. Likewise, if you are due an apology which is never likely to be forthcoming, imagine you have received and accepted it.

Without saying anything further on the matter to the person concerned, treat him or her as if all is forgiven and neither of you have any further grievance. This simple adjustment in your head relieves you of all further responsibility in the matter. It also helps to relieve anger, guilt (if you have any) and pain. You feel better and the other party cannot believe that you can be so reasonable.

The beauty of doing these exercises is that you let go of years of debilitating emotional energy of a negative nature and prepare yourself adequately for the frustrations of life to come.

David M Hinds

40

Taming fear

I HAVE OFTEN BEEN AFRAID, BUT I WOULD NOT GIVE IN TO IT.
I SIMPLY ACTED AS THOUGH I WAS NOT AFRAID,
AND PRESENTLY THE FEAR DISAPPEARED.

—Theodore Roosevelt,
26th President of the United States

Taming fear! This sounds *scary*. Admittedly, it's not the easiest of things to do, but, since you've made it this far, I think you will find the challenges ahead to be more manageable than you might suppose. Later, towards the end of the chapter, we are going to have some fun at the expense of someone who once put the fear of God into you. After that, you will be in a position to gauge just how much progress you are already making. And that's before we get into therapy in Part Five.

If we gathered up all the fearful thoughts that exist in the mind of the average person and looked at them objectively, we would see that the vast majority of them are useless.

Fearful thoughts take many different forms: we become afraid of situations in which we might make a fool of ourselves in front of other people or in which we might fail to live up to our personal expectations or the expectations of other people; we avoid certain people, situations and activities; we enter into a predictable rut and then become afraid because we know we have let ourselves down again. This cycle of self-destructive energy—from ourselves to ourselves—can have devastating consequences; it has the effect of bringing to fruition the self-fulfilling prophecy: you become so afraid of losing control that you do lose control.

In order to face down fear, we need to face the 'deathbed' test. You can do this right now by asking yourself, what are my worst fears? Then, simply ask yourself, will I fear these things on my deathbed? Our immediate answer is to say yes. But if we think about it, we may find that the thing (or things) we fear most today, we would not even remember at the end of our lives.

Now that we have established that in all probability you wouldn't give these fears the time of day in the fading twilight of your life, let's get into the routine of taming fear in everyday life. Here are some guidelines to help you in times of despair:

Confronting fear

An effective way of taming fear before it has a chance to creep up on you and get a grip is to develop your own plan for what to do when fear threatens. In order for you to achieve this, it will be helpful for you to sketch out two plans:

Plan A reminds you that you still have the option to go on making yourself miserable and depressed by rolling over and letting your fears terrorise and torture you as you did in your days of outmoded thinking. The idea behind this plan is to make you aware of how you will feel if you decide to do nothing, if you decide by default.

Plan B is just the opposite. This plan shows you how you can take precautions so that you do not become frozen with fear when confronted by a difficult situation or someone who used to frighten you. This plan brings your new powers of revised thinking into play and you refuse to dwell on matters that might otherwise depress and defeat you.

In this plan, for instance, whenever fearful thoughts try to invade your mind, you may decide to switch your thoughts to a happy occasion, one that gave you much pleasure. When confronted with someone you find difficult to deal with, you may decide to make use of the following routine.

Taming fear through comedy

With this simple technique, you can teach fear a thing or two about the overwhelming power of comedy. This mind game is a defensive strategy to be deployed when someone else is directing anger or abuse at you and you might otherwise have become fearful or in danger of losing your temper. Be careful! Do not laugh at the angry person during this routine.

Imagine that the angry or abusive person standing before you is either stark naked, or dressed only in their underclothes.

As the person's voice begins to rise, and the anger or abuse escalates, try to imagine how ridiculous he or she would sound if music were accompanying this verbal onslaught.

Try to imagine what sort of childhood and upbringing this naked or near-naked specimen must have suffered to end up an adult like this.

Congratulate yourself for remaining calm and in control. You're the winner!

Avoiding the panic button

In the process of learning new and unfamiliar survival skills and at the same time recovering from depression, there are bound to be setbacks, times when you don't get things quite right and it all goes momentarily pear-shaped. *Don't press the panic button* and give up on these proven techniques—they will work for you if only you give yourself a chance to win.

Imagine that you are a reasonably competent cook and you have just had one of the very latest and most sophisticated ovens delivered to your home. Would you really expect to produce your finest roast on the first attempt? Of course not, but perhaps you would after a little experimentation and a few setbacks along the way. These state-of-the-art life skills you are learning now take a little getting used to as well—just don't give up!

41

Getting active

ACTION IS CONSOLATORY. IT IS THE ENEMY OF
THOUGHT AND THE FRIEND OF FLATTERING ILLUSIONS.

—Joseph Conrad, Nostromo

One of the most obvious signs of depression is that we become less active. Everything seems to be such a chore and since we get little or no satisfaction from what we do, we tend to do nothing, allowing ourselves to become stagnant. Many years ago, when I was depressed, I remember spending more time thinking about life, than living it.

When we are on a downward spiral, there is a tendency to think about everything first, then to deliberate on our deliberations, then concern ourselves with the problems of our deliberations until, in effect, we are too exhausted from all this thinking to do anything at all, and so we don't. Action becomes out of the question.

There is a well-documented heaviness to depression—lethargy in the extreme—a disabling sluggishness that sucks and flattens our normal 'get up and go'. We can feel helpless and alone as if we have been transported to a planet with ten times the gravitational pull of Earth. It is this overwhelming heaviness that makes the mere thought of exercise less than delightful for many, and a real challenge for some.

It would greatly help your recovery if I could tempt you into a little gentle exercise. The key to success is to do a little bit every day, starting today.

Unless there are any medical reasons why you should not exercise, such as heart trouble, high blood pressure, unexplained pains in the chest, dizziness, fainting, or a bone or joint problem that could be made worse by exercise, I am going to ask you to give your recovery a major boost by putting down the book for a few moments at the end of the next paragraph and getting active.

Without any further thought or deliberation, I would like you to do one or more of the following: do some gentle stretching exercises on or in your bed, take a brisk walk or run on the spot until you become just a little breathless. Alternatively, a few press-ups, perhaps, or whatever you can safely and comfortably manage in the way of exercise. Please accede to my request now, before continuing with the chapter, unless there is a medical or overriding reason why you should not.

After an active break

Are you a little breathless? If so, well done. The hardest part of any programme for getting fit and active is the first part—getting started—the bit you have already completed! From now on, things are going to get easier and you are going to feel better for taking some daily exercise. Nothing too daunting, just a little a day to keep depression at bay. If you were not ready or able to take some exercise (I know, some days it can feel impossible to do what must be done) why not try again tomorrow? You can easily catch up and you will at least begin to sample a feeling of wellbeing.

Exercise has proved to be effective in:
- Clearing our minds and enhancing levels of concentration.
- Reducing insomnia.
- Improving muscle tone.
- Rejuvenating our immune systems.
- Improving digestion.

- Stimulating blood flow and vascular circulation.
- Regenerating skeletal joints.
- Building up stamina and reducing fatigue.
- Decreasing cholesterol levels.
- Lowering blood pressure.
- Strengthening our heart and lungs.
- Cleansing our mental, physical, and emotional systems.
- Strengthening our respiratory system.
- Preventing coronary heart disease.
- Burning calories and helping to keep our bodies in good shape.

When we do something that requires an element of physical exercise, we awaken a part of ourselves that otherwise lies dormant. The problem, when we are depressed, is getting started in the first place. If this is your problem, an effective way to overcome inertia is to make a deal with yourself that you will do something for ten minutes only, before deciding if it is really as undesirable as you feared. If it is, you can then give yourself permission to quit. What often happens, I find, is that after ten minutes the inertia is overcome and it is easy to keep going.

42

Quality sleep

GOD BLESS THE INVENTOR OF SLEEP, THE CLOAK THAT COVERS
ALL MEN'S THOUGHTS, THE FOOD THAT CURES ALL HUNGER...
THE BALANCING WEIGHT THAT LEVELS
THE SHEPHERD WITH THE KING.

—Miguel Cervantes, *Don Quixote*

The most wonderful thing about quality sleep is the joy of waking up refreshed and restored and feeling energetic, alert and full of life. Sadly, this is seldom the experience of the depressed person, who is more likely to snatch intermittent patches of sleep between periods of anxiety and feel exhausted and lifeless upon awakening.

One of the most infuriating and frustrating problems in life is the inability to fall asleep when we retire for that purpose. Although most of us can tolerate the occasional night of sleepless torture, insomnia that stems from anxiety or depression tends to repeat itself on a regular basis. The more you can't sleep, the more anxious you become each night because you feel you won't be able to fall asleep easily and, sure enough, it becomes a self-fulfilling prophecy. The next night, there you are again—frustrated, wide awake and even more debilitated than you were before.

A good night's sleep (or adequate rest at some other time if you are a shift worker) is essential to combat depression and to keep us healthy. We sleep in different ways at different times of the night. One of the most important types of sleep is called Rapid Eye

Movement (REM) sleep. It comes and goes throughout the night and takes up about twenty per cent of our overall sleeping time. During REM sleep our brain is active and our eyes move quickly from side to side as we dream.

The rest of the time, during non-REM sleep, the brain is less active and hormones are released into the bloodstream to facilitate essential self-maintenance and repair work throughout our bodies. Physical changes are taking place at the same time. For instance, blood pressure drops and our breathing and heartbeat slow down.

Lack of sleep adversely affects our overall mental and physical health: our heart, brain and digestive system all suffer as a direct result of sleep deprivation.

When we enjoy quality sleep, we are largely unconscious or unresponsive: we lose sensation along with our short-term memory and the ability to think properly. Sleep comes of its own accord, it does not occur in response to anything specific that happens to us but it can, nonetheless, be induced by a relaxed frame of mind. This, of course, is the problem: how do you achieve a relaxed frame of mind?

Some people find that listening to soothing music is effective; some find a hot bath helps; others prepare themselves for a good night's rest by making love to their partner or taking the dog for a walk. For me, a mug of hot chocolate is the answer.

A comfortable bed is, of course, a pre-requisite for quality sleep, but the position in which you choose to sleep can make a difference. Lying on your back with your arms at your sides is considered the healthiest position because it maintains the spine and neck in a neutral position and keeps joints stable but relaxed. However, if you are prone to snoring, your partner might complain or give you a little nudge in the night to wake you up.

Many children sleep well on their front, but for adults—particularly if you carry extra weight around your tummy—it can cause neck or back pain in some sleepers. Many people find the foetal sleeping position on their side to be a favourite choice because it keeps the airways open and is generally regarded as comfortable and a healthy sleeping position.

If you wake up in the night, try a different position.

If something is troubling you and there is nothing you can do about it before retiring to bed, make a note of the problem on a piece of paper with a view to dealing with the matter tomorrow. No longer do you have a cloud of anxiety hovering over your pillow, you have an entry on a piece of paper instead. Now you can relax, and dream peacefully. You may find—*this sometimes works, and often, it doesn't, so you can't rely on it, but it's beautiful when it happens*—your subconscious mind mulls over the problem while you're sleeping and a solution pops up in your mind when you wake up.

43

Positive imagery

WHETHER YOU BELIEVE YOU CAN OR CAN'T, YOU'RE RIGHT.
—Henry Ford

Positive imagery is about visualising precisely what you want from life. How can you be certain that you will get what you visualised? My experience could be useful. In the 1980s my life was going nowhere. I had so many problems and, seemingly, no hope of any solutions to them. Then, in desperation, I turned to positive imagery, which is a specific form of visualisation—knowing what you want in life and seeing yourself in that role until it really happens. Within a few short years I had solved all of my problems and my life was back on track and going in a worthwhile direction, the direction I had visualised.

Although some of my closest friends and my financial adviser had warned me that my intentions were not viable, I allowed myself to do what I really wanted to do, which was to study stress management and, when qualified, to set up in practice as a consultant. Within a few short years, I was chairman and chief executive of the UK's largest stress management group with ninety-two franchised consultancies.

Again, in 1995—the year that I experienced two strokes and lost everything including my health, my house and my business—it was positive imagery that I used to get back my life. As I stared up at the ceiling from my hospital bed, partly paralysed on one side of my body and unable to speak properly or comprehend the meaning of words, I visualised myself fit and well and writing a book. Five years later, I was one hundred percent fit and my first book *After Stroke* was published by Thorsons here in the UK in 2000, HarperCollins in America in 2001, and an exquisite Japanese language edition was published by Sun Choh in 2002.

And then, to my delight, an Arabic publisher – Jarir Bookstore – obtained the rights to publish my latest book, *Beat Depression*, in Arabic.

Enough about me, let's consider your best way forward, but first a little explanation and theory is called for.

Your conscious mind works rather like a spotlight of awareness, highlighting some areas of your immediate existence, while ignoring others. What you pay attention to and how you respond is determined largely by what matters most to you in a given situation. If you know what you want in life and imprint that vision time and time again on your mind through positive imagery, that spotlight of awareness will become trained and tuned to highlight aspects of life that will enable you to get what you want. Similarly, if you think only about how depressed you are, that same spotlight of awareness will focus on every possible reason and piece of evidence to confirm depression.

Give some thought in the next few days to what it is that will make your life meaningful and fulfilled. Don't just say, 'lots of money' or 'winning the lottery', because all the money in the world will not necessarily make your life meaningful or fulfilled. There are more than enough depressed and suicidal millionaires in the world to ram that point home.

If you single-mindedly want to do something particular in life, see yourself in your mind's eye already doing it. Visualise yourself doing whatever it is that you have an overwhelming desire to do or to achieve. Supercharge your emotions with thoughts and images of what it is you are going to do. Should you be one of the many millions of people in the world who cannot visually summon up mental pictures in their mind, don't worry—thinking about your dreams and intentions with real passion and enthusiasm will get you precisely the same result. Or you could draw them or paint them. This works well for some people.

Positive imagery is a technique to lend reinforcement to the thinking process and it is part of the powerful procedure to remodel your brain.

When would be the ideal time for you to practise positive imagery? Try it directly after your daily SOS session from chapter 37 on the subject of thought stopping strategies when your mind should be more relaxed and open to development. But any time to suit you is fine with me. *Now, for instance?* Later, in Part Six, we will move on to your particular purpose in life.

44

Greater self-esteem

THERE'S ONLY ONE CORNER OF THE UNIVERSE YOU
CAN BE CERTAIN OF IMPROVING, AND THAT'S YOUR OWN SELF
—Aldous Huxley, *Time Must Have a Stop*

Self-esteem starts right here, right now.

Most people assume that self-esteem is a God-given gift, but it is not—it is a quality which can be learned and that is exactly what you're going to do now. Very few people feel completely happy with themselves all the time and this is no bad thing because we all have a tendency to make mistakes and say things we don't mean from time to time. If we had too high an opinion of ourselves we would not be able to accept when we are wrong and adapt or apologise accordingly.

If, however, you are lacking in self-esteem, if you have little pride in your own ideas or abilities, you effectively cut yourself off from experimenting with new ideas and getting to know interesting people. It is obvious to others from your body language, even before you open your mouth, that you have little regard for yourself. How can we change this unflattering self-image? We can start by beginning to have some respect for ourselves and by taming that arch enemy of self-esteem—doubt!

In your dreams you are able to do some remarkable things. You can be in two different places at the same time, walk through walls, get along with all of your friends and associates and have passionate affairs with whomsoever you please. You can do all these things and more in your dreams because you don't doubt yourself.

In our waking state, most of us spend a tremendous amount of time and energy doubting ourselves. We question our self-worth and our capacity to do what needs to be done. We doubt our ability to overcome rejection, to make new friends and to win the heart of the person we want. We are using doubt in its most damaging and negative form to beat ourselves up. Of course, it makes sense to have a healthy respect for the positive side of doubt—avoiding hare-brained decisions and actions—but if we can learn to eliminate the downside of doubt and start trusting in our natural abilities, we become a new person, one to whom others are attracted.

When you get right down to it, people with high self-esteem are men and women who are comfortable and at peace with themselves. They are genuinely happy with the way their lives are progressing, regardless of whether they are serving drinks or writing bestsellers. They appear to have a strong presence because they are completely absorbed in the moment. In conversation with such people, you get the impression they are interested in you as a fellow human being. His or her mind isn't drifting elsewhere; all their energy, enthusiasm and interest is focused right there on you. Notice how they have a tendency to say pleasing, complimentary things that court popularity. They will ask about *you* because they know that your world revolves around you and, like the rest of us, you love to be flattered.

After many years in stress management consultancy, helping people to embrace and overcome problems in their lives in order to beat depression, it is clear to me that the easiest way to feel good about yourself is to make someone else feel good. Do something good for someone else once in a while without seeking reward or recognition. I have learned the truth in the saying: 'what goes around, comes around'. Whether it's taking the trouble to congratulate someone for a job well done, offering support and encouragement, a friendly phone call, an unexpected favour or something more substantial, you will feel good and, over time, your self-esteem will become greater.

What I am about to ask you to do now and every time you are alone in the bathroom for the next thirty days, may strike you as downright ludicrous, but I want you to do it anyway. Why? Because it works! Stand tall and proud in front of the bathroom mirror and say the following words with authority, sincerity and conviction.

'I am a good person. I value myself.'

Many people hold themselves in low self-esteem and become depressed because they have few friends. If this sounds like you, you will need to implement two changes in order to make a favourable impact on your present circumstances: one affecting your basic thought processes, the other concerning your social behaviour. The latter is simplicity itself and will be great fun, and the former may well prove to be easier than you think because by the time you have completed this book and the integral exercises along the way, you will already have achieved the changes necessary for success, which include:

1. A subtle but important change in the way you think about other people so that you genuinely believe (as opposed to *think you believe)* that you want to get to know them.

2. Actually getting out there with the intention of *meeting* more people (instead of *seeing* and *ignoring* them). Most people are not psychic. If you want something, you are much more likely to get it if you ask for it. Call someone you know, or visit them, to make a date for coffee, shopping, a drink, a visit to the library or gym, etc. It could become a regular thing. There's safety and comfort and increased possibilities in numbers! As you progress further through this book, your self-confidence

and your self-esteem are both destined to improve, so there is no need to dismiss this suggestion out of hand.

If you don't know anyone, telephone a few of your favourite charities and offer a few hours of your time each week for free, perhaps as a street-collector. The chances are you will meet some very kind and warm-hearted people and, in time, it follows that you may be invited to some social get-togethers.

Here are some useful guidelines

- *Avoid* being stand-offish. If you sit with your arms and legs crossed, or tightly clutching a glass, bag or plate, your body language shows that you feel uncomfortable and closed to communication, giving a clear message to others to 'keep away'.

- *Do* sit or stand where others can see you. When talking make frequent eye contact and occasionally gesture with your hands in a relaxed way (with your wrists and palms open and upwards, rather than clenched into fists).

- *Do* introduce yourself to others, rather than wait to be introduced—even if you are feeling nervous. You may be looking into the eyes of someone who would love to make you feel at ease.

- *Do* smile. The action of smiling, even if it's not sincere at the outset, actually lifts your mood and gives out a powerful and highly appealing body-language message: *I like being me—and maybe I am going to like you too!*

45

Friends

*WE HAVE FEWER FRIENDS THAN
WE IMAGINE, BUT MORE THAN WE KNOW.*

—Hugo von Hofmannsthal

I'll get by with a little help from my friends.

This chapter is addressed mainly to friends and relatives of the depressed. As a rule, I start each chapter of my books with an appropriate quotation. This time I must open with two: the one we have just read, which is so poignant and relevant to those of us who are ill and depressed; and the quotation that follows by Anais Nin, the French-born American writer of novels and short stories. On first reading her words, they can sound a bit grandiose, over-dramatic even, but over the years I have come to realise they are pertinent in every respect: *'Each friend represents a world in us, a world possibly not born until they arrive, and it is only by this meeting that a new world is born.'*

There is no doubt in my mind that my life has been enriched and broadened (and humbled at times) by the idiosyncrasies of my various friends. Quite apart from the thrill, excitement and pleasure of their company, there is the reassurance and contentment of simply being amongst friends that is an integral part of their tried and tested companionship. I have done many things (not all of which are to be recommended) that I would never have dreamed of doing if it were not for one or other of my friends.

In a perverse sort of way, I consider myself fortunate to have suffered a couple of strokes, not least because it was a telling opportunity to discover who my real friends were. Not surprisingly, after losing virtually everything including my health and my wealth, my fair-weather friends were nowhere to be seen, but my real friends (the ones who take me for who and what I am—the good, the bad and the outrageous!), they made it clear, in their own different ways, that they were there for me.

Do you know someone who is depressed? This could be your moment to do something helpful and compassionate for a friend, or a future friend, in need. Arrange to meet and encourage them to talk about their worries, their fears and about what they think might have caused their depression in the first place. The important thing here is to *listen,* to discuss possible solutions and sources of support, but to avoid telling them what to do or imposing a solution upon them. If they have not already been to see their doctor, encourage them to do so. You could offer to go with them. This can be tremendously supportive for depressed people who don't know which way to turn and lack the clarity of thought and momentum to do anything constructive to help themselves. You could present them with a copy of this book, but not *this* copy. You're on the home straight but you are by no means finished with the book yet. The best is yet to come.

During the five year period that it took me to completely recover from my second stroke, I used to wonder why on earth some of my hard-working friends with busy lives of their own would travel hundreds of miles over a weekend to cheer me up, and then travel all the way back home again. At the time, this seemed to me to go way beyond the call of duty for even the closest friend, but there is no denying that their efforts provided a much-needed boost to my self-esteem, which had suffered a series of knock-backs.

Sadly, so many of us wait until we need something from someone before we take the trouble to get to know him or her. Not surprisingly, we are frequently disappointed because when we need something from someone and they know it, they are bound to be on their guard, defensive even, because for the sake of their own self-respect, if for no other reason, they have to be able to determine whether or not we are sincere.

Another observation that is guaranteed to terminate a potential friendship prematurely is jealousy. Let's be candid here. Have you ever found yourself secretly wishing that someone else would foul-up and fail? If we are going to offer genuine and lasting friendship we must be prepared to delight in the success of others—even when that puts us in the shade once in a while. It's important to know that there is more than enough success to go round. If you have yet to taste your share of success, I have good news for you. You are working your way towards the chapters that can make all the difference to your future success and happiness. You are almost there.

Some special friends, usually older and wiser ones, have the potential to be mentors as well as friends. Typically, the ideal mentor to a person prone to depression is somebody who enjoys sharing his or her own ideas and who is both constructive and supportive, in addition to being a good, non-judgemental listener. Who do you know among your circle of friends and acquaintances who might be pleased and touched to discover you value them so highly that you would ask them for their assistance? When you have fully recovered from depression, you might wish to reciprocate his or her kindness by doing something similar for someone else.

46

Food for thought

TELL ME WHAT YOU EAT: I WILL TELL YOU WHAT YOU ARE.
—Jean-Anthelme Brillat-Savarin, *The Physiology of Taste*

Minor changes in your eating habits can lead to major improvements in your mental and physical health.

There has been much academic and scientific debate throughout 2017/18 on the effect that bacteria in your gut has on mood. The very latest research suggests that the vast ecosystem of organisms that lives in our digestive systems might be as complex and influential as our genes in matters of mental health. The connection between our gut, our brain and our mood is certainly much stronger than I had realised.

Scientists refer to the connection between our gut and our brain as the gut-brain axis. Neurotransmitters in our gut travel along our nerves and through our immune system to our brain, creating a two-way street of communication. Both mental and emotional stressors, along with biochemical stressors communicate directly through the gut-brain axis, which explains why stress can make you feel sick.

A balanced diet with plenty of exercise is the sure-fire way to keep the gut-brain highway flowing freely but the benefits of probiotics, which are friendly bacteria, can improve your mental health and your physical health and I personally recommend them as part of a healthy diet for people with depression.

Probiotic foods include the following: Yoghurt, Kefir, which is a fermented probiotic milk drink, Sauerkraut, Tempeh, Kimchi, Miso, Kombucha, and good, old-fashioned Pickles.

What you eat on a regular basis not only affects your day-to-day health, it can be instrumental in determining the quality of your life later on, how long you will live and whether or not you will become prone to illness and depression. Sadly, just when a balanced, wholesome diet is of prime importance, many people in the grip of depressive illness neglect their nutritional needs.

Some depressed people find they have very little appetite for food at all, while others go on binges or develop cravings for carbohydrates. As a result, many of us who are depressed may suffer from nutritional deficiencies or imbalances—particularly a lack of B vitamins and vitamin C, together with a shortage of the essential minerals: calcium, copper, iron, magnesium and potassium.

The finest way to correct a deficiency of vitamin C is to get stuck into some exotic fruits, together with some really juicy, fresh oranges. For some strange reason, oranges, tangerines and mandarins seem to have the added bonus of turning me off chocolate, which is a major plus because chocolate is the last thing you should gorge when depressed.

Nutritional guidelines from the Department of Health offer pointers for sufferers of depression: plenty of wholegrains and pulses and regular amounts of lean meat, oily fish, shellfish and eggs will supply B vitamins, iron, potassium, magnesium, copper and zinc. A high intake of fresh fruit and vegetables (such as asparagus, broccoli, cabbage, melons, berries and oranges) will supply vitamin C in abundance. Dark-green leafy vegetables will increase levels of calcium, magnesium and iron; dried fruit will provide potassium and iron, while low-fat dairy produce will further boost reserves of calcium.

Overdosing on caffeine (more than four cups of coffee or six cups of tea a day) can exacerbate depression because caffeine can have the effect of contributing to sleeplessness. Readers should be aware that symptoms of caffeine withdrawal—headaches and lethargy—can last up to a maximum of three days before the full benefits of caffeine withdrawal can be enjoyed.

Eat your way healthily out of depression

Consume more wholegrain breads and cereals such as barley, cracked wheat and oats. Choose brown bread and brown rice in preference to white.

- Include more peas, beans and lentils in your diet. Foods derived from soybeans can be particularly beneficial.
- Eat at least five servings of fruit and vegetables daily.
- Include oily fish at least twice a week, e.g. salmon, mackerel and sardines.
- Minimise saturated fats, which can contribute to high cholesterol levels. The main offenders are: full-fat milk, cheese and creams, ice cream, processed meats, takeaways and crisps.
- Use low-fat dairy products whenever possible and, provided you don't have an allergy to nuts, include them (unsalted) in your diet. Nuts contain a very favourable mix of fatty acids, which can have a positive effect on blood fat levels.
- Reduce your alcohol intake, if applicable, to no more than one or two drinks a day with two or three days per week alcohol free.
- Try reducing salt intake by cutting back on pre-prepared soups, gravies, stock cubes, bacon, sausages, takeaways, pickles and crisps. Cut down or eliminate the unhealthy habit of sprinkling table salt on food. Salt has its place in the kitchen during the preparation and cooking of food. It is a health hazard in the dining room and does little for the real taste of food when it has already been served on the plate.

47

Antidepressants

WHAT OTHER DUNGEON IS SO DARK AS ONE'S OWN HEART!
WHAT JAILER SO INEXORABLE AS ONE'S SELF!
—Nathaniel Hawthorne, *The House of the Seven Gables*

Worldwide drug sales for antidepressants alone exceeded ten billion pounds in 2017. Sales of this magnitude stimulate massive investment in research and development and a new generation of antidepressant drugs is on its way. Benefits to consumers will include an improved range of Selective Serotonin Re-uptake Inhibitors (SSRIs) that will move on from Prozac and its successors, bringing improvements in mood without the side-effects of earlier antidepressants which can include dizziness, dry mouth and changes in behaviour.

Currently, there are many people who are reluctant to take medication of any kind to combat depression, especially mood-altering drugs. There are fears that antidepressants may prove addictive and, in some countries, the public have been frightened by reports of tranquilliser addiction and people have become wary of anything they perceive as having a similar effect. These reservations and fears need to be taken seriously but the current generation of antidepressants are less likely to lead to addiction or dependency.

The majority of people with depression gain relief with the original drug prescribed, but in the unlikely event that you experience unacceptable side-effects, you should tell your doctor, and an alternative drug may be suggested. Antidepressants are not all the same and in a minority of cases the only effective way to find the one that brings maximum relief with minimal side-effects is by trial and error.

I see no advantage in giving complex and potentially confusing information to readers about Tricyclics, Monoamine Oxidase Inhibitors (MAOIs), and Selective Serotonin Re-uptake Inhibitors (SSRIs), when the decision to prescribe or not to prescribe is the exclusive domain of physicians. However, Prozac warrants a mention because it has become the most popular antidepressant in the world. The manufacturers claim that patients typically show an improvement in their condition two to three weeks after being prescribed the drug. The active ingredient in the drug is fluoxetine and this inhibits the re-uptake of the brain chemical serotonin, boosting chemical levels in the brain and maintaining the brain in a higher state of arousal (not depressed).

Prozac has acquired a reputation for helping people overcome not only their basic symptoms of depression, but also a range of other problems that, until recently, were traditionally thought to require psychotherapy or counselling, such as lack of self-esteem, fear of rejection and extreme sensitivity to criticism. The drug is often prescribed for senior citizens with depressive symptoms because older people are considered to be able to tolerate the same starting dosage as younger patients, which is not the case for some drugs.

So much for getting on, how about getting off? Obviously, your doctor will advise you but here are the general principles: suddenly, as opposed to gradually, discontinuing any form of antidepressant treatment can have serious consequences for a very small minority of users and there is always a risk of some minor withdrawal symptoms.

Choose the ideal time to gradually scale down your dosage as a preliminary to withdrawing from the drug altogether. A period when something exciting is happening in your life is the perfect time to quit. At the very least, ensure that things are moving your way and you have a definite and absorbing interest in life. In the unlikely event that you 'land heavily' and experience the flulike symptoms caused by too-rapid cessation of the drug, all is not lost. You simply return to full dosage for a short period, and then, by arrangement with your doctor, you progressively scale down your dosage to zero over time.

A final word – an important one – on the subject of medication. Although antidepressants can help you through an episode of depression, they cannot cure you of the condition. The best they can do is alleviate the symptoms of sadness and despair. They can't make you happy! Happiness is far more than the absence of depression. It is an affirmative state in which our lives have meaning, pleasure and purpose. More about happiness and how to secure lasting happiness later in the book.

48

Cognitive behavioural techniques

WHENEVER TWO PEOPLE MEET THERE ARE REALLY SIX PEOPLE
PRESENT. THERE IS EACH MAN AS HE SEES HIMSELF, EACH MAN AS
THE OTHER PERSON SEES HIM, AND EACH MAN AS HE REALLY IS.
—William James

A great many people think they are thinking when they are merely rearranging their prejudices.

'I think therefore I am,' wrote Descartes, the French philosopher and mathematician, in 1641. Our thoughts have a major effect on the way we perceive ourselves. At a basic level of consciousness, we are our thoughts and the content of those thoughts—whether positive or negative, loving or bitter, happy or depressed—has a direct impact on our emotions. Just one thought can have a profound effect on how we perceive the world.

To a greater or lesser extent, we act on the strength of our emotions. Because of this, the thoughts we have can influence the quality of our lives, our behaviour and our relationships with others.

In my view, based upon many years of counselling highly stressed and depressed clients, the most important factor in bringing about positive and highly beneficial changes in mood and behaviour, is exercising control over the birth of our own thoughts. The most powerful antidepressant drugs in the world cannot change an individual's underlying approach to life, but cognitive behavioural techniques of the type featured in this book can bring about lasting benefits.

This is possible because you can acquire an antidepressant skill you can use again and again without the need to rely on doctors and drugs. People who employ cognitive techniques find that their behavioural patterns change and they approach life more constructively; problems are more easily solved and life is more enjoyable.

Here are two real-life examples of cognitive behavioural therapy in action. The first case concerns Mary, a woman in her forties. You are not Mary, and your circumstances are not hers, but this case study will have served its purpose if you are moved to consider what it is that may be wrong, missing, undesirable or self-destructive in your own life.

Bear in mind that bitterness, betrayal, anger, loss, perceived failure and the desire for retribution and revenge—each of them classic ingredients for depression—can all show themselves in many different ways. The underlying root cause, the personal factors contributing to your own depressive illness, and the keys (actions necessary) for self-release, will, of course, be different to Mary's, but the possibilities for recovery can be just as good.

Mary's husband had been unfaithful at an office party. It had been a one-night stand, he had sworn never to do it again and she believed him. Yet, she could not forgive him: she was outraged by the betrayal. She had no desire to leave him—besides, they were Catholics and divorce was out of the question—but still she went on, day after day, night after night, punishing him, making herself more and more depressed.

I was disappointed at her lack of progress over a period of many weeks. She was making things worse for herself, not better. Her husband, having been forced by Mary to resign his previous job, had started a new one on the very day of the session I am going to tell you about, thus bringing to an end a dismal twelve-month period of unemployment. By her own admission, Mary had been difficult, nagging her husband incessantly, instead of treating this as an opportunity for a new beginning. Somehow, she had to be encouraged to think and act differently. I was in no doubt that subtlety was no longer an option.

'Mary, do you still love your husband?'

'Yes.'

'You do want this marriage to work?'

'I do.'

'Now this bit is not easy, but the time has come for you to forgive your husband.' I had no intention of breaking the silence that followed. She was going to respond, even if we went into extra time.

'I can't,' she admitted at last. 'I want to, I know I have to, *but I just cant do it!*'

'I have a simple technique for you, Mary, to make it possible, and I am going to give you the opportunity to practise it with some homework, and I require your word of honour, here and now, that you will complete it to the very best of your ability'

'What is it that you want me to do?' I believe she was pleased I had acknowledged the fact that if she gave her word, she would keep it.

'Do I have your word? Without it we have nowhere to go.'

'Of course!'

'Have you got a clock on the mantelpiece at home, Mary?'

'Yes.'

'Can you see it from your favourite chair?'

'Yes.'

'Good. Now this is what I want you to do. Go home and relax. Look at the base of the clock and direct all of your resentment for your husband's betrayal towards that one spot. Concentrate like never before. Visualise yourself transferring every last drop of venom out of your heart and under the clock, secure in the knowledge that it will be there tomorrow, waiting for you, should you wish to retrieve it. Are you willing to give this a go, Mary?'

'Yes.'

'Next, I want you to prepare a special candlelit dinner with wine just for the two of you. Today is a cause for celebration for you both. Your husband has started his new job and you are about to take a great leap forward. Put on your most seductive dress and make love to him tonight. That is your homework, Mary. Same time next week?'

The next time Mary walked into my consulting room, I felt proud of her. She looked younger and even her complexion somehow seemed softer and smoother. There was sparkle in her eyes where before there had been only pain, mist and haziness. We didn't really need to say much. Life was going to get better and she and her husband were going to have peace of mind.

The details of this case are unimportant; the important thing is to distance yourself from the bitterness and resentment of the past and to think about the way forward.

The second example of cognitive behavioural therapy in action concerns myself. At the beginning of 1995, I was the chairman, chief executive and founder of a nationwide group of ninety-two franchised stress management consultancies, enjoying the fruits of my achievements: satisfaction, life in the fast lane and a rather grand lifestyle. By the end of the same year, I had virtually nothing, not even my health. Two strokes in August had left me brain-damaged with the carotid artery to one side of my brain destroyed.

On the plus side, my somewhat dry sense of humour had not deserted me and I knew a thing or two about stress management.

Using the same cognitive tools that I am teaching you, I succeeded in convincing myself that the only thing that mattered was getting well after the two strokes, one of which rendered me paralysed down one side of my body. Twenty-three years on, I have reclaimed both my health and my happiness and succeeded in winning the heart of the most wonderful woman who is now my wife

49

The ultimate challenge: forgiveness

And forgive us our trespasses,
as we forgive them that trespass against us.
—The Lord's Prayer, from the *Book of Common Prayer*

Crucial to your recovery—*forgive yourself* as well!

Forgiving is by far the most difficult undertaking I shall ask you to attempt in this book. I know, from my own life experiences, past and very recent, the exercises towards the end of the chapter will test you. Nevertheless, if you really are to recover from depression, if you are to go on to enjoy a happy, meaningful life, I cannot spare you now: you are too tantalisingly close to achieving a monumental step forward in life. Second only to the ability to love, forgiveness is the greatest test of our qualities as human beings.

The only way to heal the pain that will not heal itself is to forgive the person who hurt you. Not forgetting to forgive yourself at the same time for any complicity, omission, or personal responsibility in the matter. Forgiving erases the intensity of the hurt from your memory and allows you to move on. When you release the wrongdoer from the wrong, it's as if you are cutting a malignant tumour out of your inner self. You set a prisoner free, but you discover the real prisoner was you.

In demonstrating that forgiveness can positively enhance emotional health, Professor Carl Thoresen of Stanford University in the United States of America, lead researcher for the Stanford Forgiveness Project, has said, 'Very few people understand what forgiveness is and how it works.'

What is forgiveness?

Forgiveness is the act of cancelling an emotional debt from the wrongdoer to you, and from you to yourself. It involves a conscious and deliberate process of revised thinking to bring about this total transformation of feelings from bitterness and resentment (or even hate) to feelings of genuine compassion. These humanitarian emotions allow your heart to open up and become receptive to the extraordinary act of will and courage necessary to complete the forgiveness exercises later in this chapter.

What if I am not yet ready to forgive?

If you are still reading, then clearly you have reached the stage whereby you are at least **prepared to contemplate forgiveness** even if you are not ready or able to forgive just yet. Already you have come a very long way along the path towards forgiveness. I cannot believe that you will persist in torturing yourself for ever now that relief from all that pain is almost within your grasp. Forgiveness is something that you can prepare to do despite your misgivings. Forgiving is a process that has a very definite start to it and you may be closer to the starting line than you thought possible days—even hours—ago. The start is deciding that in the end you will forgive, you will recover; you will have a better quality of life.

Why is reconciliation so hard after conflict?

Depressed people have particular difficulty in achieving reconciliation after experiencing hostility—whether it occurred either a week or more than fifty years ago. In the majority of instances, this is because as children we were never taught how to reconcile our differences with other people and now, as adults, we feel awkward about acquiring the skills to go about it.

Another reason so many people feel that they cannot contemplate reconciliation is their need to be proved right, to have the moral high ground, the dominant position. The person who reaches out to make peace is perceived as the one who has submitted. This, by implication, infers that he or she may have been the one in the wrong. This is sad, because the one who reaches out, the one who tries to heal the rift, regardless of right or wrong, is very likely to be the finer character.

It can be even harder to forgive someone who is dead. Or someone who isn't sorry for what they have done, or someone who is blissfully unaware of the hurt they have caused. Quite possibly, the offender did not deliberately set out to hurt you. Parents and children, lovers and sweethearts, husbands, wives, in-laws or ex's know a lot about this.

Forgive yourself: life didn't come complete with a step-by-step instruction manual for getting it right every single time.

We are human, and this implies that we are going to make mistakes, mess up, lose our way, say things we regret and be downright selfish and unbearable once in a while. I am not a religious person myself, but I believe the most wonderful thing about saints is that they were human. Like us, they may have lost their tempers, got angry, scolded God, made mistakes and regretted them, but still they were awarded the 'Peace of God', which, to me, surpasses all understanding.

So, what is the big deal about getting things wrong from time to time? Why are we so hard on ourselves? Why cannot Mr, Mrs or Ms Perfect accept that life is a learning curve and that there is much to be gained from accepting our weaknesses and forgiving others and ourselves?

The core texts of the world's principal religions recognise that the quest for happiness is not without its challenges and obstacles.

The experience of fulfilment would seem to involve some kind of spiritual journey through life, which at times appears almost to go beyond the limits of human emotion and understanding. Depression is a tragedy by any standards, but much good can come out of it if we are persuaded to address a matter which is long overdue: forgiving ourselves and others who have wronged us.

Doing it

There are three straightforward steps to forgiveness: Step 1 is dissolving resentment; Step 2 is identifying with the wrongdoer's possible motivation in a compassionate way; Step 3 is the act of forgiveness itself, which is forever irretrievable. You can't wake up tomorrow and decide to rescind it. Please note, the sequence and contents of these exercises are exactly the same regardless of whether you are forgiving yourself or other people.

STEP 1: Dissolving resentment

Sit quietly, close your eyes and relax. Imagine yourself sitting alone in an empty, dimly lit theatre. You can sit in the front row, the back row, in a private box, or anywhere else you choose as long as you place the person or persons you are going to forgive on the stage. It could be someone from the past or the present, living or dead. It could be an image of yourself up there on the stage while you remain in your seat.

When, in your mind's eye, you see this person/these people, imagine wonderful things happening to them, the sort of things that would make them happy and contented without in any way threatening or saddening you. See their smiling face/s fill with delight and feel the warmth of their happiness touching you. Hold this image for a few moments, longer if you wish, before opening your eyes.

You can repeat this step daily, with a different person or group of people. Should you experience difficulty in visualising images in your mind, you can instead paint, draw on paper or create these scenes on your computer.

I want to, but... I just can't do it!

If you really can't overcome your resentment and find it in your heart to forgive, you must realise that it is your recovery that is at stake. If you cannot forgive the person who hurt you, you must dismiss him or her from your mind. See them as beneath contempt if that helps, and move on. Don't allow such a person to get in the way of your recovery.

Forgiveness is the only option in the end, but if your hurt has been so deep that you cannot deal with it without thinking of revenge, use the following technique:

Resentment workout: revenge

Skip this step if possible. Use only if necessary. Use only once. For some of us, even nice people, there is an unsavoury but necessary interim step to take before we can feel able to bring ourselves to forgive. Sometimes, a part of us needs to have revenge before we can move on. OK, let's get on with it.

Close your eyes, relax and think of all those people (or that one particular person) who are (is) hardest to forgive. What would you really like to do with them if you could have your way with each and every one of them? In your idea of a perfect world, what would you have them do to earn your forgiveness? Imagine it happening, play it through in your mind, enjoy it, savour it, and now get down to the details. Exactly how long do you want them to suffer for, and how much should they suffer? When you are satisfied you have worked through your resentment, that's the time to get down to the serious business of forgiving—yourself included.

STEP 2: Understanding and identifying with the wrongdoer's possible motivation in a compassionate way

Try very hard to be compassionate in your thoughts of the other person. Bear in mind that they were probably trying to do the best they could with the limited resources and abundant problems they had at the time. Their priorities and values may be different from yours. Identify with the person's possible motivation and try to think of charitable reasons for the motivation behind what they did, or what they said, that hurt you so much. If you were responsible for contributing to the situation in some way, admit it, learn from your mistake, then release yourself and the other person from the situation once and for all.

STEP 3: The act of forgiveness

Sit down, stand to attention or kneel, whichever seems appropriate to you. Close your eyes and say these words out loud, 'The person I need to forgive is... (name) and I forgive them for... (state succinctly what they did, or said, to hurt you).'

Repeat this three times, each time with increased emphasis, conviction, and absolution in your voice, and in your heart.

Well done. Now you can really concentrate on getting better and *you will succeed*.

PART FIVE

Therapy

50

Therapeutic thoughts

> Our life is what our thoughts make it.
> —Marcus Aurelius

Treat yourself to the luxury of some nice thoughts!

Praise is the most wonderful tonic. It is not of paramount importance whether the uplifting message you receive is praise from someone you admire, from a complete stranger, or self-praise (congratulating yourself for refusing a chocolate, resisting the urge for yet another cigarette, or for motivating yourself to do the housework or to get up and take a walk). What matters is that the spotlight of your mind focuses on something good, something reassuring, and something nice about you, instead of languishing in the dark shadows of depression.

When we are depressed, we feel under-appreciated, as if no one, including ourselves, understands how hard we are trying to piece together the fragments of our lives and lift ourselves off this island of isolation. At times like this, it is important to stop what we are doing and give ourselves a pat on the back for a genuine achievement, regardless of whether it is a great stride forward in our recovery, a minute but measurable step in the right direction, or a kind action for someone else.

Take a few moments to reflect on what you have been doing to improve your situation and don't forget to give yourself a huge helping of well-deserved praise for reading this book. This book may well be easy to read, but it's not easy to read and respond to when you are depressed. You are doing that right now and I admire you greatly.

Take time out at the end of this chapter to congratulate yourself on your recent and past achievements and give some recognition to the special attributes you possess and the kind deeds you have done in your life. Think about what you have just read. Contemplate only the good things about you and your life for a while. Do this, and I believe you will begin to bring the hint of a smile to your lips and a lump to your throat. Okay, so life has been mighty tough for a while now, but there are quite a number of things that are special and nice about you, aren't there?

Recognising our contribution ourselves can actually be more powerful and satisfying than hearing it from others, although, naturally, we love to hear those (rare) wonderful words of praise from loved ones, associates or the boss.

Sometimes, in the maelstrom of modern life, and particularly in the depths of depression, it is all too easy to forget about the worthy contributions we make to ourselves, our families, our friends and the people and businesses that we work for or did work for in the past, together with the donations we make to charities in terms of time or money.

Without doubt, each of us has something to commend ourselves for and many of us have so much for which to pat ourselves on the back that the occasion of finishing this chapter really ought to be a moment (or perhaps an evening) of celebration. A celebration of ourselves and the good things we have done, or tried to do.

I operate what some people would regard as a bizarre and silly system of non-existent gold stars but it works for me so why would I care what other people think?

Whenever I finish a chapter, or walk up that particularly gruelling hill that is situated near to my home (I don't do hills very well these days), or do something else worthwhile or beneficial to my health, I award myself a mythical gold star. They don't actually exist; I just conjure them up in my mind, but to me, they are valuable because I never award myself one unless I deserve it. *Daft, you may think?* Well, actually, no, not daft. I derive great pleasure at the end of a busy day counting my gold stars and congratulating myself.

51

Music therapy

IF MUSIC BE THE FOOD OF LOVE, PLAY ON.
—William Shakespeare, *Twelfth Night*

Harness the power of music to comfort your soul.

Music possesses that special quality capable of making us uniquely aware of our innermost feelings. Somehow it becomes acceptable to shed tears while listening to a sad or moving song, the very same tears we struggle to suppress when confronted with our own or another's pain.

Music, as you will experience in the following exercise, can have an extraordinarily powerful effect in exploring and exposing the hidden motivations for our darkest moods and most private melancholy. It can function as a catalyst for discovering, soothing and disentangling deep-rooted sadness and internal mayhem.

Through music, we can recall the past, live the present and prepare for the future. Music has a wonderful—but sometimes daunting—ability to freeze images into recollections, releasing them later in life as images. As children, we dream of being adults. As adults, we dream of having our childhood again: the same childhood for some, a different one for others.

Music, as John M. Ortiz illustrates brilliantly in his book *The Tao of Music* is a very powerful stimulus. Whenever music is associated with a particular moment, event or personal experience, the listener can attach very private imagery, feelings or personal meaning to that particular piece of music. Later, through music, one is capable of re-experiencing a mental and emotional representation of the essence of the moment when it was first heard. Sometimes, you play the music just to experience that moment once again.

In this short chapter you are about to learn how to harness the power of music to affect your own mood. If you ever wanted to be a record producer, this is your special moment. You are about to accomplish something far more important than producing a number one album, you are going to produce your own real-life music soundtrack that encapsulates special significance and meaning for you.

The result of your efforts will resonate deep within your subconscious mind and produce a therapeutic effect upon you. Your proposed music therapy recording will consist of a compilation of sounds that have hidden connotations for you. It will help you to connect and get in touch with your depressive mood and move on from it. In order to proceed from this point you will need some form of recording and playback device.

Get out your entire music collection! Don't hesitate just because you are feeling sceptical about the potential usefulness of this venture, just immerse yourself in choosing music that has distinctive memories for you and put them into three categories as follows:

Sad and lethargic

Choose several songs or pieces of music that best seem to capture your depressed state. Many depressed people find their choices for this category of music tend to be melancholic, slow-tempo numbers. Certainly, they should be tracks that have made a powerful impression on you in the past. If I were masterminding a compilation album for myself, the Righteous Brothers' recording of 'You've Lost That Lovin' Feelin'' would come immediately to mind.

Moody, changeable, mid-tempo

Now choose a selection of songs or pieces of music that best seem to match your mood when you are neither particularly happy nor sad—just OK. Again, they should be tracks which hold a special meaning for you.

Upbeat, happy, electrifying!

For your final selection, pick recordings that take you back to your happy moments—the real high spots in your life. Many people find these are often tracks with a fast, vibrating tempo, music that is alive and bursting with passion and enthusiasm.

Take as much time as you need over your selections. For some, this assignment will be a rather enjoyable, whole-day occupation. When you feel you are ready, place your selections in order of extremes of mood from melancholy at the beginning to happy at the end (which, coincidentally, is how you would *like* to feel) and record them that order.

Play several times a week for a few weeks and experience for yourself what music therapy can do for you. Over time, you may find your predominant mood moving distinctly away from the sad and miserable low point of depression you have been experiencing of late, hovering for a while in a more comfortable 'changeable to Okay' frame of mind, before lingering for longer, *much longer*, in the happier emotions of life.

On the subject of happy emotions for me personally, one of the great joys of life here in the UK is listening to the radio station, Classic FM. They play some real gems!

52

Dance therapy

DANCING, I BELIEVE, LIKE VIRTUE, MUST BE ITS OWN REWARD.
—Jane Austen, Emma

Dance is a tonic for the heart as well as being highly beneficial to body and spirit.

Dance is one of the oldest therapies known to man and yet it is only in recent years that dance has become an accepted therapeutic tool. Dance has the capability to lift dulled and depressed individuals out of their everyday tedium and to get their under-active bodies moving and stretching in time to the music. To a large extent it does away with the necessity for one to think or talk and it allows many alienated people to come together since dance can be a social outlet as well as a therapeutic tool.

One of the great joys of dance therapy is that it doesn't really matter whether you can do it properly or not. Lack of a convenient or willing dancing partner is of little significance either. I remember in the days when I was partly paralysed, fully depressed and striving to recover from the aftermath of my two strokes, I would put on some music and dance my way around the flat with the upright vacuum cleaner in an effort to get myself active and to make some impression on the household chores.

If you are by yourself, the ideal way to lighten your mood and get active is to select a piece of music with a good range of dynamics, something that starts slowly and builds up to a powerful crescendo.

If necessary, move the furniture out of the way and allow your body, not conscious thought, to dictate your movements. There is no need to be self-conscious or to try to impress anyone, least of all yourself, just move to the music and let your hands and feet take over.

Dancing to your favourite choice of music is an excellent way to combat the blues, to defy depression, and to get the dusting done if you happen to have a duster in your hand at the same time. It can give real lift to your system even when you are feeling exhausted. Like exercise, once you get started, it triggers an exuberant rush through your body that can quickly jog you out of your black mood or distract your depressed train of thought.

Dancing is becoming ever more popular within many different age groups. If you can't dance too well but would like to go to a dance, don't worry about looking silly—the idea is to enjoy yourself with others, not to show off in front of them. If you think you would be too self-conscious to enjoy yourself, join a beginner's class where everyone will be at the same level and you can improve together, probably making some great new friends at the same time.

Whether you prefer dancing in nightclubs, discos or parties or prefer folk or ballroom dancing, you're getting really good exercise for your body and a fabulous lift for your spirit. Dancing is excellent for banishing the blues, improving stamina and increasing the strength of your legs. It can also help your joints remains supple and mobile and it's particularly good for your sense of balance—mind, as well as body!

Dance is not only an ideal way to get active, reduce tension and forget your troubles; it is a tonic for the heart as well as being highly beneficial to the body and spirit. It allows us to be moved by something other than depression and, if persisted in, can help to restore the soul and lighten the burden for those of us who are having a really hard time.

David M Hinds

53

The talking therapies

CONVERSATION HAS A KIND OF CHARM ABOUT IT,
AN INSINUATING AND INSIDIOUS SOMETHING THAT ELICITS
SECRETS FROM US JUST LIKE LOVE OR LIQUOR.

—Seneca

'It's comforting to know there is someone working constructively with me to overcome this setback.'

My experience in treating depressed clients either as individuals or as participants in my 'Beat Depression' initiatives and 'Tackling Under-Performance' workshops for companies has left me in no doubt that the talking therapies have an important part to play in beating depression, but now scientists have proved that depressed individuals can be livelier, happier and more productive after just six sessions of psychotherapy.

A total of twenty-eight seriously depressed patients aged between thirty and fifty-three were monitored with SPECT (Single Photon Emission Computed Tomography) brain scans to check blood flow during a study commissioned by the Royal College of Psychiatrists in the UK. Fifteen patients were then given a six-week course of antidepressants and the remaining thirteen were given six one-hour sessions of interpersonal psychotherapy. After six weeks all the participants' brains were scanned again.

Brain scans could show whether the patients felt better because when they talked about their troubles the blood flow increased through the part of the brain that is believed to be responsible for depression. The scans on the group of fifteen people undergoing treatment with antidepressants showed a marked increase in blood flow to specific areas of the brain during the trial period. The scans on the group of the thirteen receiving psychotherapy also showed a dramatic increase in blood flow to specific areas of the brain. The effect was similar to that achieved by antidepressants, but therapy also managed to affect a part of the brain untouched by drugs.

Those who had received psychotherapy also showed a marked increase in activity in the area of the brain thought to control body movements and co-ordination. Stephen Martin, a consultant psychiatrist at Cherry Knowle Hospital in Sunderland, said: 'This is the largest study ever done using brain scans in sequence to monitor depression. It's fantastic to see that we have got some areas of the mind switching on in sequence in the same way as with medical treatment. Certainly, talking works. The conclusion is that patients do best with a combination of structured therapy and antidepressants. I think the process of being listened to is important, but there is good evidence that interpersonal psychotherapy is a lot more effective than just talking. It's not a quick discussion—it is quite intensive work linking the patient's depressed mood with their problems and helping them with quite strong direction from the therapist.'

The patients involved in the study had all expressed symptoms of major depression at the outset, including sleep disturbance, weight loss or gain, fatigue and feeling unable to enjoy life. A survey six months after the study found that none of the patients had relapsed.

Every depressed person needs someone to talk to. Actually finding such a person, someone who really understands, is incredibly comforting and empowering. In those rare moments when we feel able to give voice to our confused and despairing thoughts, the greatest gift we can hope for is to have someone with the capacity to listen, who can gently and objectively help us make sense of our muddled ramblings, to show us—with especial sensitivity—the next step forward. I am convinced that this is why the talking therapies are so effective in helping people beat depression.

54

Laughter

The world is a looking-glass, and gives back
to every man the reflection of his own face. Frown at it,
and it will in turn look sourly upon you; laugh at it
and with it, and it is a jolly, kind companion.
—William Makepeace Thackeray, *Vanity Fair*

Laugh and the world laughs with you; laugh and depression is in retreat.

Healthy young children laugh as many as four hundred times a day, the average adult manages fewer than fifteen laughs daily, and the clinically depressed are hard pushed to manage one decent laugh all day. These figures are disappointing when you consider that a good laugh can defuse tension, relieve stress, elevate mood and draw the sting from the agonies of social embarrassment.

The mental and physical health benefits of humour are well documented in a public health study conducted by Dr Lee Berk in California. One hour of naturally induced laughter significantly lowers levels of the stress hormones cortisol and epinephrine and stimulates the body's cells and antibodies.

Years ago, long before the first of my two strokes, I remember reading a quite remarkable book by the American journalist, Norman Cousins, titled *Anatomy of an Illness*. In it, he tells of his painful struggle with a life-threatening spinal condition. He knew, from personal experience, just about everything there was to know about pain and he was aware that laughter had the power to release the body's natural painkillers, endorphins, into the bloodstream. One weekend, when the pain was monumental, he checked into a hotel, complete with a suitcase full of *Candid Camera* and *Marx Brothers* videos, and proceeded to test the therapeutic benefits of laughter. Cousins discovered that five minutes of spontaneous laughter (not polite, not restrained) gave him up to two hours of pain relief. And, despite his chronic condition, he felt better about himself and life in general.

In order to successfully humour our away out of depression, we shall need a strategy to escape from the emotional trough in which many of us find ourselves from time to time. One way to achieve this is to create a secret inner world of fun and frivolity, just like we did as very young children.

All of us have to live in this less-than-ideal world and our inner environment is the only one over which we can exercise any real control. We can help ourselves to cope with the ups and downs of life by developing our own personal sense-of-humour trigger. Here's an easy way to go about it: the object of the exercise is to be able to see the funny side of every situation that might otherwise upset you. During the evening, or last thing at night, is the ideal time to do this exercise.

Loosen your clothes and take off your shoes, relax your body and let the events of the day fade away. Take three slow, deep breaths and recall a happy moment from your very early childhood. For a few blissful moments you are going to be a child again.

Consciously force yourself to bring a smile to your face and summon the child from within you. Recall an incident from today that has (or could have) upset you and become, once again, the child you once were. Call on the child within you to poke fun at the incident in question. Change the facts of the matter and the ending to please yourself, just as if you were writing your own novel. Give it a funny ending, one that pleases you and makes you laugh.

55

Pet therapy

ANIMALS ARE SUCH AGREEABLE FRIENDS –
THEY ASK NO QUESTIONS, THEY PASS NO CRITICISMS.
—George Eliot, *Scenes of Clerical Life*

For some people, acquiring a pet can be the beginning of a magical partnership, and the act of ownership can mark the beginning of the end of depressive illness. In Great Britain alone, around seven million canine chums now share human homes and no fewer than eight million purring moggies are currently providing their owners with snug companionship.

Cats and dogs are more than just man's best friend. Recent studies have demonstrated that pets can help their owners in a variety of ways, including the lowering of blood pressure, improving mood and speeding recovery from depression and other illnesses. For example, heart attack patients who own pets are five times less likely to suffer a second heart attack within a year of the first, than patients who don't own pets.

Just having a pet around has been shown to reduce stress and improve the owner's general sense of wellbeing. In residential care homes, visits from animals have been shown to reduce depression and increase alertness in elderly people with dementia. People with physical disabilities can also benefit tremendously from having a pet. The sensuous and enjoyable act of running your hand over a dog's head, patting its side or tickling its tummy can be a different but rewarding physiotherapy exercise for those with limited arm movements.

Naturally, it is important for potential owners to realise that pets have feelings and needs as well. They have a moral right to be well cared for and looked after, to be kept healthy, fed and well nourished. Some potential owners, living in small flats in built-up areas and unable to get out much, might worry that, if they did get a pet, it might not be happy. Obviously, in the circumstances described, a little kitten, or a cat, would seem to be more practical than a dog.

It could be amusing to devise new ways to keep the little fellow entertained. With a kitten, encourage him to play with objects that he can investigate, such as a toy mouse. Provide cardboard boxes that he can climb into, cushions he can hide under, and possibly a cat climbing frame or activity centre. The pair of you will probably enjoy great fun, companionship and happiness together. Furthermore, the comfort and unconditional love provided by a warm, furry creature is often the precursor to being able to feel human tenderness again.

56

Hot baths and mind games

IT IS THE HEIGHT OF LUXURY TO SIT IN A HOT
BATH AND READ ABOUT LITTLE BIRDS.
—Alfred, Lord Tennyson, Said upon having
hot water installed in his new house

The thrust of this book was conceived in a hot, leisurely bath.

Some people haven't taken a bath for years! In this high-tech, energy-efficient age, millions of people miss out on the therapeutic benefits of a hot, leisurely bath in preference to a quick shower. Edmund Wilson, the noted US critic, had this to say about my favourite early morning routine: 'I have had a good many more uplifting thoughts, creative and expansive visions while soaking in comfortable baths in well-equipped American bathrooms than I have ever had in any cathedral.'

The purpose of this chapter is to prepare you for an important exercise that we shall address in detail later. With this aim in mind, I must tempt you into the bathroom for a luxuriously long and uninterrupted hot bath, complete with a generous measure of a relaxing, aromatherapy bath essence.

The bath essence ideal for the simple but empowering mind game we are going to start to play in this chapter is a blend of two essential oils: geranium and rosewood. If you are traditionally more of a 'last thing at night' person in the hygiene department,

I can assure you that this particular bath will do much more for your recovery and sense of wellbeing than an evening in front of the television or surfing the Internet.

It is essential for you to be able to relax comfortably in the bath for this session of self-therapy. If you don't have a headrest to lounge back on, place a couple of fluffy towels on the ridge of the bath for you to rest your head on. This is quality time we are looking for here, not a rapid scrub and an out-you-get quickie! You won't be in the mood to do what is required of you if the kids (grown-up or the tiny variety) can come barging in on you, and please turn off any radio, TV or loud music that could disturb the session you are about to embark on.

Relax and enjoy the luxury of your hot bath with the mind-soothing aroma of geranium and rosewood. When your mind is calm, allow your thoughts to wander to what it is that you would do with your life to make it meaningful if there were no restrictions whatsoever on your right to happiness. When you get out of the bath, note down your thoughts. We shall be referring to them later.

57

Massage

I LIKE A MAN WHAT TAKES HIS TIME.

—Mae West

Experience, or remind yourself of the power and importance of touch.

Massage has been shown to reduce blood pressure and alleviate some types of headache. It has been used effectively in the treatment of depression brought on by trauma. A study at the University of Miami Medical School has demonstrated that depressed patients who received the benefit of a half-hour massage had consistently lower levels of stress hormones during the massage and afterwards. Patients also reported they were able to sleep better.

One of the great joys of massage is that you are helpless on the couch with nothing to do. You have little choice but to lie back and let your therapist do with you as he or she wills. Massage releases tension, frees energy, removes physical blocks and feels good. It also brings awareness to the sensory nerves—just what you need when you are feeling depressed. Should you find yourself thinking or worrying about anything during your massage, simply abandon your thoughts and revert to the unparalleled luxury of lying there and being pampered in the name of therapy.

In the event that a commercial massage is beyond your budget, or if you would prefer to enjoy the benefits of massage alone at home, I strongly recommend you to treat yourself to the ecstasy of an Indian head massage dispensed with your own two hands. You don't need anyone else to help you to do this: you have the power to melt away pain and relieve stress in your own fingertips.

Narendra Mehta, who is totally blind, devised this and other massage techniques in India and brought them to the West. In his truly brilliant book *Indian Head Massage—Discover the Power of Touch*, he recommends the following self-administered method of head massage (please note that advice given in this chapter is not suitable for persons suffering from any chronic or acute health problems, such as whiplash injuries, migraine, epilepsy, psoriasis or eczema; if in doubt, please consult a doctor or professional therapist):

Relax; sit down comfortably in loosely fitting clothing with both feet on the ground and prepare to experience how a firm rub about the skull can relieve tension and how soothing strokes to the top of the head can give the sensation of lifting depression. Now follow these simple instructions:

Gently massage the whole of the area of your scalp with thumbs and fingers, releasing any tension by friction and rubbing.

Grasp fistfuls of hair at the roots and tug from side to side, keeping your knuckles very close to the scalp.

Squeeze at the temples with the heels of the hands and makes slow, wide circular movements.

Look down slightly and massage the back of the neck by squeezing and rolling the muscles. Start at the top of the neck and work your way down, first with one hand and then with the other hand. Repeat this a few times.

How do you feel now? Great, isn't it? Why not get into the habit of treating yourself to a head massage more often? You'll sleep more sweetly at night if you do.

58

Swimming with dolphins

THE DAY I SWAM WITH DOLPHINS, I BELIEVE I WAS REBORN.
—Bill Bowell

An unlikely therapy—swimming with dolphins—is proving remarkably effective in treating psychological illness. Horace Dobbs, founder of the Oxford Underwater Research Group, director of International Dolphin Watch and a former atomic scientist, reveals in his book *Dolphin Healing*, that interacting with dolphins can have a therapeutic effect on those suffering from depression. 'A dolphin can communicate moods that we can't define scientifically,' explains Dr Dobbs. 'One of the reasons why I believe humans have this special relationship with dolphins is that, in us, they recognise their cerebral partners. Dolphins rely on two senses, sound and vision, both of which are many times more complex than the human equivalent. They have the ability to carry out ultrasonic scans in their brains, which makes them highly sensitive to human emotions.'

Researchers have discovered that some dolphins break away from their habitual groups to become what scientists have described as 'ambassador' dolphins. These creatures are usually bottle-nosed dolphins and predominantly male. They live alone in their chosen territory and appear to prefer the company of humans. It is these dolphins, the evidence suggests, that have the ability to heal mental diseases. They have been described by sufferers and researchers alike as having telepathic skills for understanding and unlocking emotions and fears buried deep in the sufferer's mind.

A wealth of anecdotal evidence, as well as scientific studies, confirms the healing power of dolphins. Bill Bowell, a retired 65-year-old manager from Oxford, had suffered from chronic depression for years after having a heart attack at the age of fifty-three.

'Depression is such a devastating disease both for the sufferer and for the family,' he said. 'I was unable to work for twelve years because of it. I was a recluse, paranoid, aggressive and suffered from self-loathing. Doctors put me on several antidepressants over the years and I was assigned to psychiatric counselling, but nothing worked for me.'

Three years ago, Bill was lowered into the freezing waters of St Bride's Bay, off Solva in South Wales. 'My life changed for ever. I was petrified. I could barely swim and I was shaking like a leaf as the grey shape of a dolphin approached me from below.

'After I spotted him, he slowly crept up and lay beside me in the water. He looked straight into my eyes for a few minutes, and I burst into tears. I was mesmerised and my emotions erupted like a volcano. As I cried, he rested his head on my chest and stayed very still. Finally, after ten minutes, I reached out and touched him. He nudged my face and tickled my ribs until I laughed out loud.

'It was a moving experience and one I will never forget. Since then I have swum with dolphins on several occasions. I am now fully recovered: I take no medication and have returned to work. I am finally able to talk to my children again after almost ten years of barely knowing who they were.'

There are countless other stories from people who claim to have been healed after swimming with dolphins and there are many reliable ambassador dolphin territories around the world. The nearest operational location near to the UK at the time of writing (January 2019) is Donegal in the Republic of Ireland. In Australia, you are spoilt for choice with loads of safe venues. Likewise, Florida, Mexico, Portugal and Dubai.

Could this be a worthwhile adventure for you? Only if you can swim, of course. In any event, Part Six: More Therapy, which comes next will be spot-on for all. No flippers required. Guaranteed!

Stop press! Hold everything. Do you believe in miracles?

I tend to break-off from my morning's writing around eleven-ish and take a walk before lunch. On the way back, on 23rd January, passing my local newsagent's shop, I was captivated by the headline—AMAZING FOOTAGE CAPTURES DOLPHINS IN PLYMOUTH SOUND—complete with a half page picture of the dolphins on the front page of my local paper, the Herald, in my adopted home city, Plymouth.

I called the paper at once because I wanted that picture for my readers. It was taken by drone by videographer Lewis Huddy, the director of *Heads Up Definition*, a professional drone company here in Plymouth. The picture follows courtesy of © Lewis Huddy. But I do not recommend to readers that they swim with dolphins in Plymouth Sound among the plethora of yachts, fishing boats, continental ferries, Royal Navy warships and nuclear submarines!

David M Hinds

PART SIX

More Therapy

59

The default settings of your mind

WE KNOW WHAT WE ARE, BUT KNOW NOT WHAT WE MAY BE.
—William Shakespeare, *Hamlet*

One little change of mind can unlock the deadlock.

You will recall, at the commencement of chapter thirty-five, I introduced you to a gentleman who is regarded as the father of neuroscience, Santiago Ramón y Cajal, the joint Noble prize winner in Physiology or Medicine in 1906 in recognition of his work on the structure of the human nervous system. He was the neuroscientist who said, "Any man could, if he were so inclined, be the sculptor of his own brain." And, of course, he was absolutely right, although I tend to refer to the process as *remodelling the brain*.

Don't be intimidated by the fact that the process sounds rather grand. The outcome will be excellent although the actual steps to accomplish it are very simple and explained in stages over a series of upcoming chapters. Basically, all we want to do is alter the default settings of your mind from *'depressed'* to *'no longer depressed'* so that you can get on with your life, enjoy it, and make the best of it. This is a straightforward procedure that you will need to learn, practise, and then put into practice.

The end result will be a bit like having a ready-made toolbox in your head for automatically dealing with life's problems as they present themselves. You will be equipped to cope; you will know how to use the toolbox. Some people and many practitioners refer to some of the techniques we shall be covering as cognitive behavioural therapy or CBT for short. That's accurate up to a degree, but there are differences of a technical nature, which need not concern us for now because I want to return to a familiar theme of mine: the analogy between the human mind and a computer.

For the benefit of those who are not computer buffs, I should point out that if you tell a computer to do something it will continue to do it until you tell it otherwise. For instance, if the setting on your computer is pre-set to leave one space after a full stop, like this. That is what you will get unless it is specifically altered to leave two or more spaces.

One can parallel this with the mind of a depressed person—their tendency will be to follow the same pattern of thought and not be capable of lifting themselves out of depression. Their pattern of outmoded (negative) thinking must be replaced by a revised way of thinking which will lead them to recovery. In other words, the 'default' setting in the mind must be altered to make progress.

To achieve this, it will be necessary to switch from outmoded to revised thinking at the birth of our thoughts, at the very moment they enter our conscious awareness. That is what we shall be doing in the next two chapters and it will not be difficult. It will be fun, and then, *we're off on an adventure!*

60

D-thoughts

Great thoughts come from the heart.
　　　　　　　　—Marquis de Vauvenargues,

Defuse D-thoughts. D-thoughts are depressing thoughts.

Before we successfully adopt a concept different from the one we are accustomed to, I find it helps to first know what *not to do*. With revised thinking, the concept by which you are going to banish depression and bring laughter, happiness and opportunity into your life, it is crucial to defuse D-thoughts! D-thoughts are dangerous thoughts, and we don't want any more of them.

Not only are D-thoughts dismal, dangerous and depressing, they are disabling as well because they drain you of the power to choose today how you will feel. For instance, if you lose your job, you could succumb to a wave of D-thoughts and despair at the prospect of ever getting another job. This is natural but the important thing is to move forward to the position where you can regard this enforced change as an opportunity to get a better job, downshift, or start an enterprise of your own.

The essential difference between these two thought patterns— the one, outmoded thinking and the other, revised thinking—is the absence of D-thoughts: the self-deprecating thoughts that immediately spring to mind if you let them.

D-thoughts should not be confused with the irritation and disappointment we feel when things go wrong, or the natural grieving process we experience over the death of a loved one. D-thoughts are an entrapment of mind born of habit in hard or threatening times and they lead us into a crisis of despair and hopelessness. They condition us to expect the worst and we must learn to stifle them at birth so that they cannot drag us down into depression and keep us there. We will find out how to do this in the next chapter but, first, let's see just how destructive D-thoughts can be...

According to a study published in the *British Journal of Psychiatry* the death of Princess Diana caused an alarming increase in the suicide rate throughout England and Wales. The increase was especially high among young women. Analysis of official government figures has revealed that the suicide rate jumped by almost a fifth (17.4 per cent) in the four weeks following her funeral.

The researchers, led by Professor Keith Hawton of the Warneford Hospital, Oxford, also found that cases of attempted suicide, including drug overdoses and other deliberate means of self-harm, increased by 44 per cent the week after Diana's death, with hospital admissions of women up a staggering 65 per cent.

The main contributing factor in almost all depressive illnesses and suicides is negative thinking—D-thoughts! In the next chapter there is a technique for defusing D-thoughts that anyone, from a child to a pensioner, can get to grips with. You are about to revise the default setting for your mind and to reach for recovery.

61

The revised setting for peace of mind

GREAT EMERGENCIES AND CRISES SHOW US HOW MUCH
GREATER OUR VITAL RESOURCES ARE THAN WE HAD SUPPOSED.
—WILLIAM JAMES

It's time to switch from outmoded thinking to revised thinking.

Ivan Petrovich Pavlov who received a Nobel Prize for his work on the digestive system and conditioned reflexes, is the Russian physiologist who is going to help me to make the concept of revised thinking supremely easy for you to understand.

The most famous of Pavlov's experiments were his studies on the behaviour of dogs. He would ring a bell and then feed the dogs. He repeated this procedure many times over a period of weeks: he rang the bell; the dogs salivated and ate the food. After a time, the dogs would salivate at the sound of the bell—even when no food was available. He described their response to the bell as a conditioned reflex: bell, salivation, food.

This type of reaction—responding instantaneously to a stimulus—became known as the 'Pavlovian response' and it was the source of Pavlov's insights into human behaviour. Our basic human thought processes, Pavlov found, work in much the same way and this is why it is sometimes necessary to revise the default settings of our minds, that is to say, the stimuli that set us off on the wrong track.

When we hear the bell, we don't want to salivate when no food is forthcoming. Likewise, we do not want to think the worst when the worst is not necessarily the only thing on offer. Sadly, many of us have unconsciously conditioned ourselves in depression to do just that, ignoring all other happier options by default.

As humans we can make ourselves aware that such stimuli are false, that we do not have to make the conditioned response. We can be aware of falling into the D-thought trap and turn away from it.

Our perceptions determine what we actually experience in any given situation because they make us receptive to some stimuli and blind to others. Those of us who expect to find problems in a given situation are usually able to find them, while those of us who expect to find opportunities in the same situation will also be successful. In order to revise the default setting of your mind from unhelpful D-thoughts to positive, forward-looking thinking, I am going to ask you to do three things. The code name I use for the process you are about to undertake is SS30.

1. Stop! Every time you catch yourself thinking a negative, depression-inducing D-thought, you should dismiss that thought immediately from your mind by thinking of Pavlov's dogs salivating at the mouth, before switching your thoughts to something good, satisfying and positively in your favour. Your revised thought can be anything pleasing you like: a fond or happy memory from the past or a promising thought about the future, but absolutely no D-thoughts of any kind! For example, if you need help but find it difficult to ask for help, think how you feel when someone asks for your help and you give it. You feel good, don't you?

2. Suspend any disbelief in the effectiveness of this process for a period of thirty days. Please do exactly as I ask, even if you feel far from optimistic about the outcome right now. I want you to get well and I know you can do it.

3. Thirty days is how long it can take to make or break a habit or to revise the default setting of your mind. To be certain of success, you must keep on banishing D- thoughts from your

mind every second of every minute of every waking hour for thirty days. Don't worry; it becomes easier by the day! Very soon you will be a revised thinker. You will have succeeded in resetting the default setting of your mind and you will beat depression.

62

Adventure at any age

WHAT YOU CAN DO IS LIMITED ONLY BY WHAT YOU CAN DREAM.
—Dick Rutan, Voyager pilot

Some people believe we have many lives and that this one is merely for practice purposes. Religious people believe they will go to heaven. I believe we get only one innings and everyone owes it to himself or herself to find out how to make it as worthwhile and enjoyable as possible.

We are never too old to get it right and even if we do have another chance in another life, wouldn't it be nice to know that we succeeded in turning our life on earth into a great adventure? We don't need money to achieve this; all we need is a sense of adventure.

Your life has the potential to be a wondrous journey, filled with exciting moments and astonishing experiences. It can be thrilling and deeply satisfying only if you are keen to explore all that is available to you. It doesn't matter if your life has been misspent or a bore to date, what matters is the change for the better you are prepared to make as a direct result of reading this book. You have everything to gain; make the nightmare of depression a positive turning point in your life. This option is red-hot, enticing and open to you. Only you can slam the door by default, by doing nothing to please yourself.

Are you interested in taking up this option? Good, here's how to overcome one of the two remaining hurdles standing between you and your depression-free life of the future. Answer the following question: what is it that gives you real satisfaction? What makes you spark? If you don't know, but you are willing to find out, you could be in for an even greater adventure; you may need to try many things in order to find out what really does it for you!

An adventure is any experience that takes you beyond your comfort level. Adventures are different things to different people, but they are invariably experiences that make your blood race and your heart beat with anticipation as you expand beyond your perceived limitations as a human being. They enlarge your horizons and take you into new territory, on to more exciting and satisfying levels of life. At the same time they benefit your family and friends because you become a richer and more interesting person, more worldly wise, someone who it is a pleasure to be around.

What you choose to make of your life is exclusively up to you: you can either create an exciting life filled with wonder and adventure or stay huddled and safe, never experiencing the thrill of journeying outside your own private world with its in-built routine and limitations. A life devoid of adventure may be secure, but it is a life lacking in texture and colour, one that can give rise to feelings of boredom, emptiness and depression.

Living life to the full by realising our dreams and finding time for fun and adventure is something most of us could do if we were prepared to go beyond our comfort zone. Depressed people have a distinct advantage over others in this respect. They have experienced so much pain, isolation and misery in the depths of their depressive illness that the prospect of change no longer looms like a potential nightmare to them; it is salvation: something to be embraced with open arms.

All that now remains is for you to decide what it is you want to do, what kind of thrill are you going to give your well-deserving self? Will it be an adventure with the potential to be highly therapeutic, like the one in the next chapter, or will you choose something completely different? Now that you are approaching the final hurdle, all that remains is for you to leap, lurch or launch yourself into action.

63

A purpose in life

NOTHING CONTRIBUTES SO MUCH TO TRANQUILLISE
THE MIND AS A STEADY PURPOSE: A POINT ON WHICH THE
SOUL MAY FIX ITS INTELLECTUAL EYE.

—Mary Shelley

Destiny is not a matter of chance; *it is* a *matter* of choice.

Money, power, total freedom, a huge and impressive home, the hunkiest, most handsome man imaginable to satisfy your every whim or the queen of the catwalks as your personal trophy. If you had all that, and more, could you guarantee to be free of depression? Actually, no.

How do I know? The times in my life when I have experienced real satisfaction, success and fulfilment, have been, without exception, those times when I have followed my dream and set about doing what I had a genuine passion for. You should first subject whatever it is that you believe will bring purpose and meaning to your life in the future to the love test.

The love test? When considering your vocation, your purpose, your genuine passion for the game of life in which you are none other than the most important player, you must want to do it for the sheer joy of doing it, not just for the material benefits that you might reasonably expect it to provide. If your passion does not survive this crucial test, you could be mistaken in your assumption of what it is that will bring joy and happiness into your life. You may need to get more closely in touch with your inner self to realise your true destiny and to bring your dream to fruition.

The kiss in the tail of the love test, I have discovered, is that once you discover your real passion in life and go for it with persistence and determination, satisfaction comes eventually and then just keeps on coming. What's more, because you are doing what you love doing, not only is your life meaningful, happy and fulfilled, but your relationships and your interaction with loved ones become more natural and pleasing.

I could have written this book solely for the sheer enchantment and challenge of doing it, and the same applies to my first book, *After Stroke*, which in fact I wrote to give myself a reason to learn to read and comprehend the meaning of words again following the ravages of stroke illness (and, incidentally, as my way out of depression). I had no idea at the time that Thorsons would publish it on both sides of the Atlantic as an international paperback. The moral behind this and countless other success stories, similar and more spectacular, is to find your passion, that special something that means so much to you that you would willingly do it without payment—and the good things in life will then find you.

Only you can discover your purpose in life, which, for some people, may be a variation or renewed intensity on something they are already doing, something completely different, or something they had always wanted to do but never quite dared to attempt until now. Once you have decided on the new direction or the new emphasis for your life, put it to the love test and if it passes, don't be surprised if your depression fades as you plan for action.

64

Committing your purpose to paper

I FELT AS IF I WERE WALKING WITH DESTINY, AND THAT
MY PAST LIFE HAD BEEN BUT A PREPARATION FOR THIS
HOUR AND THIS TRIAL...I WAS SURE I SHOULD NOT FAIL.
—Winston Churchill

What in your power would make you proud and happy? Write it down. Plan to begin.

Before you can plan for action and expect to succeed it is a good idea to commit your new or renewed purpose in life to paper. In stress management and motivational jargon this is referred to as a 'personal mission statement'.

Life has more meaning and depth to it when we have something definite to do—a mission to fulfil—and if we fail to recognise this we run the risk of getting lost and becoming depressed should we experience bad luck, disappointment, something new that we are ill-equipped to deal with, or tragedy of any kind. By our very nature, our lives need to be dedicated to something and a crystal-clear mission statement, written from the heart and read regularly, helps to focus our mind.

If you spend your life doing what you really love doing, it stands to reason that life will be a pleasure and you will excel at what you do because you love doing it. This doesn't, of course, mean that every aspect of your life will be perfect, or even enjoyable, but it does mean that the general thrust of your life will be forward- looking, happy and fulfilling.

Many people start off with a passion for life but they lose it along the way. Perhaps you once had a passion for doing excellent work, taking risks, being creative, making friends, helping people, homemaking, childminding, theatre, exploring new ideas or possibilities or doing voluntary work for charity? Or perhaps you may have had a passion for the quiet life, or perhaps a zest for the cut and thrust of business, entertainment, adventure and travel that turned out to be less fulfilling than expected. Our priorities and passions change as we progress through life and in any event, we don't always get it right first time. I know I didn't.

Don't set out to impress yourself or anyone else with your personal mission statement. This really is your life you are going to forecast and the all-important ingredients of this statement are truth, realism and personal integrity. Whether you are sixteen years old or a hundred and six, the document you are about to prepare for your own exclusive use is of paramount importance to your future happiness.

So potentially rewarding for you is the next step, that I am about to break the rule of a lifetime. Never before have I shown my personal mission statement to anyone other than my fiancée and my mentor, but I am willing to put it before you now in the hope that it may inspire you to reach into your heart as never before and help you to prepare your own statement. Forget about all past mistakes and disasters. Get this right, and you will live a dream come true. Here is my mission statement from 1999.

David M Hinds
My Life in the Year 2000 and Beyond

I am creative and I will write some more really useful health and motivational books. I am doing this with my life because I want to and because I get tremendous satisfaction from the results of my writing. I regard the letters of appreciation from readers that are forwarded on to me by my publishers as a measure of my success. I am happy and enthused by this, my third and final career. This year I will endeavour to find someone to love and cherish who is uniquely desirable. I will be truthful, kind and faithful to her and we will be friends as well as lovers.

Why not make today the day you make a start on the next chapter of your life?

65

Balance

INSTEAD OF SEEING THE RUG BEING PULLED FROM
UNDER US WE CAN LEARN TO DANCE ON THE SHIFTING CARPET.
—Thomas F. Crum

Balance, on the tightrope through life, requires flexibility.

Depression, however frightening, is never permanent. Nevertheless, it is wise to have it treated in order to spare yourself, your family and your friends, needless pain and suffering, and to reduce the risk of suicide while the mind is unbalanced. Whether it is treated or not, depression has a tendency to disappear of its own accord. This may take a few weeks, months or well over a year, but it invariably happens. Our brain chemistry adjusts to the imbalance in the system and corrects itself—until the next time—but we ourselves can learn to get some genuine balance into our lives.

Our brains seldom tolerate extremes of emotion for long periods. Just remember the ecstasy of those heady, early days in love. You felt as though you were floating on air, unable to eat, concentrate, or think of anything but the object of your emotions. Did it last? You may well still be in love with that wonderful person but you won't be on such a high. The endorphins, which our brains create to make us feel wonderful at the birth of new love, overload, then balance out over time. Fortunately, a not dissimilar balancing act takes place in the reverse, lifting us from depression.

Lasting happiness, emotional wellbeing, and the ability to remain permanently free of depression are internal processes which are generated from within each of us. Only we can decide how best to live our lives and exactly what personal fulfilment means to each of us.

The thrust of this book has been a common sense approach to beating depression once and for all by taking full responsibility for our thoughts, our lives, our decisions, our behaviour and our mistakes. There is no mileage in the blame game anymore. We have learned how damaging and self-defeating that spiteful little boomerang can be. Instead of blaming others and ourselves for any shortcomings we may have, we are going to set about getting some real balance into our lives.

Here are some suggestions as to how to go about it:

- When you are working, give it all you've got, but be sure to spend quality time with your loved ones and make some special time available exclusively for you to do the things that you want to do.

- Live your life now. All time is real time. Don't put your life on hold waiting for a more convenient time to live it.

- Consider how much time you spend surfing the Internet, watching TV and drinking in pubs. Relaxation is important, of course, but are you doing these things to relax or because you're lonely or bored?

- If you don't like your life, or if there are aspects of it that don't appeal, make a list of the pluses and minuses in your lifestyle and set about making a plan to improve things.

- The key to a balanced life is spending sufficient time on the various components of your life: career, family, health, pursuits and hobbies, social aspects, further education, belief structures, leisure, holidays, entertainment, community affairs and charity work, etc.

- Be friendly and forgiving to those around you. Friendship is a goal worth pursuing. It means you can find a way to meet in the middle and share other people's dreams without feeling as if you are sacrificing anything. There is something very special about true friendship, something worth cultivating.

- Refer to the personal mission statement you prepared earlier in the book, amend it if necessary, and set about thinking of ways to make it happen.

- Ask yourself, 'What do I wish I had more time for?' Make it happen!

- Once in a while, do something nice, spontaneous, unexpected and totally out of character, for someone else. *Get some excitement back into life!*

Never forget that the three components of happiness are something beneficial, worthwhile or enjoyable to do, someone to love, and something to look forward to.

66

Enjoying the moment

Happy the man, and happy he alone,
He, who can call to-day his own:
He who, secure within, can say,
To-morrow do thy worst, for I have lived to-day.
—John Dryden, From a translation of *Horace*

Look until you find something promising in your situation.

Eventually, when you look back on your life, it's unlikely that you will be thinking about how much money you did or didn't make, or whether or not you got your own back on that person who crossed you. You are more likely to be thinking about the purpose of your life and the people in it who mean so much to you.

We all change as we journey through life. There was a time when I used to think that all that mattered was success and making a fortune. These days, I believe the purpose of life is to *live*, love and be loved and, in some small way, to enrich the lives of others. If your life doesn't strike you as worthwhile or rewarding, change it: it is never too late to change.

On the assumption that you are not at death's door, indulge in life. Don't put off living it until you are feeling completely and utterly better. The experience of depression is awful, but you stand to gain so much from what you've been through when you decide to act upon the knowledge and greater understanding of yourself that you now possess.

Start doing some of the things that you always wanted to do. Make your life enjoyable and meaningful and others will benefit, too.

If you want to make things difficult for yourself, you'll find all the reasons in the world why you shouldn't enjoy your life: why you should postpone enjoyment until things are different, until you have got whatever it is you want. But time is ticking away and not one single moment can be replaced. The life you have lived so far has gone for ever. You can't have it back to relive those wasted moments.

The best any of us can do is put greater value on life in future and to treasure all those remaining moments, including this one. The assumption that we will always have another moment, a moment better than this one, is flawed in one fatal respect: our lives can be changed completely in the twinkling of an eye by a heart attack, a motorway pile-up, or a stray bullet meant for someone else.

In the split second before I suffered a major stroke in my late forties, had you asked me if I was going to be seriously ill for the next few years, I would have laughed. Had you enquired a moment later, I would have been speechless. Enjoying the moment is the most wonderful concept you can adopt and it is your homework for the rest of your life.

67

Highlighting

The farewell quotation

SOME BOOKS ARE TO BE TASTED, OTHERS TO BE SWALLOWED,
AND SOME FEW TO BE CHEWED AND DIGESTED.

—Francis Bacon

Reach for your highlighting pen.

Let there be no doubt from the outset what this chapter is about. It is about extracting maximum benefit from this book by having a yellow (I suggest yellow, purely because it complements, rather than obscures, black print) highlighter pen to hand while you read, to highlight those words and paragraphs which may have particular significance for you. Why? So that you can locate them again quickly and easily, time and time again, whenever you need them for reinforcement and encouragement.

If you are reading an e-book version of this book, your choice of highlighter colour may be limited to blue on some devices, but that's fine. Anything that gets a result for you is okay by me.

Why am I telling you this now, in the last chapter?

On the first page of this book, it required only one tick to involve you in your own recovery, but even if you were only mildly depressed, that tick was not only the first step, it was a *major* step towards recovery. I had no intention at that point of complicating matters with highlighters and re-reads.

Almost everyone reads a book, even a self-help book, as if it were a novel: from front to back, seldom stopping to question and re-read those sections with specific relevance to him or her. This is fine for a first read, but within these pages are techniques and strategies that have taken me over thirty years to extract from my experiences and evolve into book form. Even Superman could not be expected to absorb all this in one read.

From my experiences of successfully recovering from both a minor and a major stroke, clinical depression, and treating depressed clients in my stress management consultancies, I believe this book will succeed in its stated aim, but seriously depressed readers will need more than one casual read. Hence the highlighter...

Whenever I read a book that I am determined to benefit from, I devour it. I read each line again and again if necessary until I have fully grasped the meaning of every word, highlighting the passages that strike me as being of crucial importance.

To gain maximum benefit from this book, to attend to all of the issues leading up to your depression and to resolve them, you must do the same: devour this book; extract all the information that could be useful to you, and then set about translating the essential principles and strategies you have learned into *action*. Recovery may not be easy, instantaneous or swift, but it will happen.

AUTHOR'S FAREWELL NOTE

This has been a book that is very close to my heart. I would be delighted to read reviews on Amazon and in the social media from readers who have benefited from the book. Likewise, I welcome comments from readers with suggestions for improvements or additions that could be helpful to readers of future editions. I wish you well and a full and happy life.

www.DavidMHinds.com

After Stroke

The Complete, Step-by-step Blueprint for Getting Better

UPDATED AND EXTENDED 2022 EDITION

DAVID M HINDS AND DR WEI FONG LIM

"*A warm and motivating read.*"
—EOIN REDAHAN, The Stroke Association

AFTER

Updated
and
EXTENDED
2022
Edition

STROKE

FOREWORD BY PROF. SIR PETER J MORRIS

DAVID M HINDS

and Dr Wei Fong Lim

Other Titles by David M Hinds

After Stroke is a motivational lifeline for all those recovering from stroke—and their carers too—helping them to adjust to this new situation.

Complete with information on risk factors; why a stroke occurs and what happens when it does; clear diagrams to help movement after stroke; how to get the best care in a specialized stroke unit; how to work hand-in-hand with the professionals; tests and surgery; and a comprehensive and valuable worldwide resource section.

Updated and Extended 2022 Edition

DAVID M HINDS, who has himself made a 100% recovery from a major stroke, has used many of the techniques he employed as a successful stress management consultant to create a warmly personal and practical step-by-step recovery plan. After Stroke is a motivational lifeline for all those recovering from stroke—and their carers too—helping them to adjust to this new situation.

The author stresses the value of the three 'P's—Patience, Positive attitude and Perseverance—and includes the following advice:

• Keep calm, stop worrying and hold on to your sense of humour

• Simplify your life and let others help. All that matters is getting well

• Balance periods of healing exertion with much-needed rest

• How the emotions you feel (anger, bitterness, guilt) can be used to fuel recovery

Complete with information on risk factors; why a stroke occurs and what happens when it does; clear diagrams to help movement after stroke; how to get the best care in a specialized stroke unit; how to work hand-in-hand with the professionals; tests and surgery; and a comprehensive and valuable worldwide resource section.

"Invaluable not only for people who have had a stroke but also for their carers." —Peter J. Morris, FRCS, FRS, Nuffield Professor of Surgery, University of Oxford

"Excellent." —Richard Madeley live on ITV's *THIS MORNING* show (03.02.2000)

David is a stress management consultant by profession specializing in problems of the subconscious mind. His latest self-help book is Beat Depression. At the time of going to press (September 2022) David's multi-award-winning screenplay titles TASER and THE HAPPINESS ANGEL are the OUTRIGHT WINNERS of 16 International Film Festival Screenplay Awards – a world record for an unproduced script. So far, he has declined all options because the right production deal has yet to present itself. He lives with his wife, Tatiana, in Plymouth, Devon.

WWW.DAVIDMHINDS.COM

ISBN 978-1-83778-005-1

£12.99

CONTENTS

- Changing position in bed
- Sitting up in bed
- Getting out of bed
- Standing
- Walking
- Relaxing safely in a chair
- Eating difficulties
- Swallowing
- Communication disorders
- Slurring of speech (dysarthria)
- Inability to speak (aphasia)
- Caring for an aphasic person
- Speech and language therapy
- Occupational therapy (OT) and home care assistants
- FastTrack ways to get better
- Exercise, diet and lifestyle changes for sustained recovery
- Driving
- Counselling
- Music therapy
- Dance therapy
- Pathways to happiness

Part Seven: Depression

- Stroke and depression
- The downward spiral of depression
- 'Black dog'
- High anxiety
- Diffusing anxiety bombs
- Anxiety blocking
- Prozac
- Death of a loved one
- A purpose in life
- Pet therapy
- Quality sleep
- Bath time
- Aromatherapy, massage, and yoga

- Break out with *Beat Depression*: the non-addictive, readable antidepressant

Part Eight: Adjustment
- Drama and tears
- Facing the future
- Self-determination
- Increasing self-confidence
- The self-fulfilling expectation
- The nursing home option
- Independence

Part Nine: Wellbeing
- Accepting yourself after stroke
- Zest for life
- Plan for recovery
- The peak of recovery
- Next generation drugs and therapies
- Robotic therapy

Part Ten: Happiness
- Courage
- Working from home
- My resolution as carer for someone special
- My resolution as a stroke survivor

Worldwide Sources of Help and Support

Foreword

I first met David Hinds early in August 1995 following his major stroke, which had been preceded, by a minor stroke a day or two before. He was referred for consideration of surgical reconstruction of the blood flow to his brain.

As you might imagine, over that few months I saw a great deal of David. He was a relatively young man who had had a very busy lifestyle and a very successful career, but who was slowly realising that his career, and even perhaps his life, was in ruins. Needless to say, he was extremely angry about this and early on unavoidably showed this in his relationships with his carers.

However, what was fascinating was that over those early weeks as all the problems that he had begun to sink in (which are so well described in this book), he began to consider how he could adjust his life to cope with his disability, and what he could do to minimise his disabilities. In this remarkable book he describes his reaction to the stroke and how he managed to cope with all the problems associated with a major stroke.

He has now made an excellent recovery and has established a new lifestyle for himself. This book is not only a record of his own experiences of coping with a stroke, but also a distillation of a vast amount of reading and discussion on the subject. Furthermore, it is expressed in a way that will make it invaluable not only for people who have had a stroke, but also for their carers.

Peter J. Morris, FRCS, FRS,
Nuffield Professor of Surgery
University of Oxford

Other Titles by David M Hinds

Introduction

Every year in Britain, more than 100,000 people have a stroke. In the United States, the figure is approaching 800,000 annually. Worldwide, 15 million people have a stroke every year. The physical and emotional impact of the illness on patients and carers is enormous. The majority of stroke patients survive but many are severely brain-damaged and disabled. The purpose of this book is to inspire and motivate the 12 million annual survivors of stroke worldwide into making the best possible recovery available to them.

For the vast majority of patients with the capacity to recover, it is possible to reclaim their health and lifestyle providing they possess the will to get well and a genuine willingness to struggle. This patient-centred book will help.

The ten parts of this book coincide with the principal psychological effects of actually experiencing a stroke. The mental response to suffering a stroke is fundamentally a grief reaction. The patient is mourning the loss of faculties, lifestyle and status.

Grief, a natural human reaction to loss, is a process of adaptation and passes through a number of recognizable stages, regardless of whether the loss is a loved one, amputation or paralysis. These stages include alarm, shock, denial, anger, guilt, acceptance and adjustment. The majority of stroke patients also go through a period of depression. Sadly, at present, too few patients and carers reach the final stages of wellbeing and happiness. *After Stroke* will steer readers towards this positive outcome.

I have personally made a hundred per cent recovery from one minor and one major stroke and a subclavian bypass operation. I hope that you will find this book helpful and easy to read. My aim is to reveal the inside story, the know-how, the essential steps to recovery, with humour, frankness and authority. I want to reach out to a stroke victim's feelings of frustration, distress and depression from the depth of personal experience, moving patients and carers resolutely onward. The book is focused on total recovery from stroke, nothing less.

Unlike any other book on stroke that I have ever read – *and over the last 23 years I've read many* – this one is designed to be easy to comprehend and comes complete with worldwide sources of help and support. After the shock and damage of a stroke the last thing you or your carer needs is a complex academic book loaded with medical terminology. *After Stroke* is served up in easily digestible bite-size chunks because I understand from personal experience the difficulties you may be going through right now.

This greatly expanded 2020 twentieth anniversary edition benefits from having the very latest medical information updated by my friend and neighbour, Dr Wei Fong Lim. He specialises in geriatric medicine having accepted a fellowship in stroke medicine in 2018. Since his training days as a medical student in Guy's, King's and St Thomas' Medical Schools in London during the early and mid-noughties, there has been a tremendous improvement in stroke medicine.

Many professions, in addition to medical research, have lent their skill and energy to the question of stroke recovery including physiology, psychology, electronics, genetics and neuroscience. However, most important of all in my personal view, has been the greater focus in recent years on educating the general public about the tell-tale signs of someone actually having a stroke and the need for an emergency ambulance to be called at once. This is because every single second of delay can mean an increasingly challenging period of recovery for the patient.

It is hard to believe that almost twenty years have elapsed since the original February 2000 Thorsons/HarperCollins edition of *After Stroke* was published. Unexpected TV interviews resulted for me with Richard Madeley and Judy Finnigan on ITV's *This Morning* show, BBC2's *Cornish Chronicles* series, and Channel 5 News. Proud moments for me in the overseas news department were that the

Japanese version of *After Stroke* had also been warmly received along with the Arabic edition of *Beat Depression* – the companion book to *After Stroke* because, regretfully, so many stroke survivors get depressed.

The really good news is that life after stroke can be great. *Yes, I mean great!* I'm happier now than ever before. It was twenty years ago, while recovering from stroke and writing the first edition of this book, that I met the woman who would later become my wife. Now, after eighteen wedding anniversaries, I can honestly state that the two of us love each other more than in those heady early days of our relationship.

Despite losing my home, my stress management consultancy business and the millionaire lifestyle that went with it decades ago as a direct consequence of stroke, my friends – a few of whom have known me for more than 50 years – marvel at how happy I am. Read on and make the best recovery available to you so that you too can enjoy a happy and fulfilled life after stroke. I hope this book will be an inspiration and offer renewed hope to you personally and your carer.

David M. Hinds
Plymouth, 15th August 2022

PART ONE
Alarm

1: You are never too old to recover from stroke

GREAT EMERGENCIES AND CRISES SHOW US
HOW MUCH GREATER OUR VITAL RESOURCES ARE
THAN WE HAD SUPPOSED.

—William James

You are never too old to recover from stroke: not everyone can make a complete recovery, but most of us, over time, can manage a major improvement in our condition. The keys to a quality life after stroke are support, guidance, rehabilitation and, most important of all, the will to get well. For those of us who are alone in the world, the will to get well can be the deciding factor.

The first ten days after stroke are the most cruel. After that, with adequate aftercare and the right attitude of mind, things can get progressively better. Make no mistake, recovering from stroke is never easy. For some it will prove to be the toughest challenge of their lives but for the chance to win back our health, with all the rewards, opportunities, and treats that will accompany success, are we not willing to do whatever it takes to get well?

Just for a moment, let us suppose that the forthcoming struggle to recover our health will be an adventure, not an impossibility. In order to understand how and why, at almost any age, we have a phenomenal ability to recover from stroke, allow me to give you an insight to what is happening inside your brain. You may be reassured to discover that your brain is quite capable of navigating around the stroke-damaged areas of itself in much the same way that you might take a detour if your usual route home was blocked by an accident. Your brain has spare capacity for emergencies such as this.

EXPRESS RECOVERY TIP
Commit to the best possible recovery you can manage.

Damage by stroke occurs only in the brain. Nothing at all has happened to the muscles. They malfunction on one side of the body after stroke because they are not getting the usual messages for movement from the brain. With time, physiotherapy and perseverance, the stroke patient who survives the initial trauma can often recover lost or impaired faculties as the brain finds alternative pathways around the damaged areas.

I know only too well from my own experiences of recovering from two strokes that you must be feeling frustrated and frightened right now. A stroke defies definition in so many ways. No two strokes are the same. Suddenly, unexpectedly, your whole life implodes. The saddest thing about stroke is that your nearest and dearest can help you but they can't enter into the struggle. No one but you can win.

Despite your misfortune, if you can somehow summon the will to read on, this book will hold your good hand and guide you every step of the way through the marvels of your own recovery. The essential first step is to commit your heart and soul to recovery, the best possible recovery that you can manage.

2: Let's cut off the blood supply to the brain

IF ANYTHING CAN GO WRONG, IT WILL,
AND AT THE MOST INOPPORTUNE TIME.

—Murphy's Law

The majority of readers of this book will be stroke patients, their carers, family and friends. If you are reading this book as a stroke patient then you are indeed doing well. *You are a survivor!* The road to recovery and wellbeing after stroke may well be a difficult one but I can assure you with absolute sincerity that it is worthwhile to struggle. Following almost total recovery from my second major stroke three years ago, I am happier now than ever before.

A BASIC UNDERSTANDING OF WHAT HAS HAPPENED TO THE PATIENT WILL BENEFIT US ALL.

Let's cut off the blood supply to the brain and simulate a stroke!

When the blood supply to the brain is interrupted, a complex series of metabolic processes takes place and calcium poisons a cluster of brain cells, accelerating their demise. At first those cells under siege from blood starvation remain alive but cease to function properly. Within four to eight minutes, irreversible damage results and cells in the affected part of the brain inevitably expire.

At the fundamental cell level, a human brain might be compared to a computer. After all, computers are essentially a series of tiny switches that can be programmed for either 'on' or 'off', depending on the task to be performed. Likewise, our brain cells (or neurons to be precise) either 'fire', discharging an electrochemical signal for some kind of action to take place (the movement of a finger, for instance), or 'do not fire', if no change is required. It is this interruption to the orderly flow of brain signals caused by defunct and damaged cells that plays havoc with one side of the body after stroke.

EXPRESS RECOVERY TIP

Hang on to your sense of humour. You'll be needing it.

Unlike the cells in the tissues of our skin or liver, which can usually reproduce those lost through damage, once an adult loses a brain cell it is gone for ever. Fortunately, most of us have a few billion of them. To get around the effects of brain damage caused by stroke, patients must try to retrain undamaged brain cells to take on new roles, such as controlling their muscle movements to facilitate walking. This can be easier than it sounds because the connections between brain cells become more sensitive close to the area that has been destroyed. Also, swelling around the grey matter in the skull will subside. When this happens, the less damaged brain cells regain their function and your recovery accelerates.

It will take time, determination and, in many cases, the intervention of a highly-skilled physiotherapist before other brain cells mirror the performance of cells consumed by stroke and mobility can be restored. For the benefit of every patient with the capacity to recover from stroke and, so important, the will, the step-by-step road to recovery is here within the pages of *After Stroke*.

3: CAUTION: brain attack

Even if the prospects seem bad,
you have to carry on.

—General Eisenhower

When the blood supply to our brain is interrupted, a 'brain attack' occurs. Usually this happens because a blood clot blocks an artery but it can be caused by bleeding directly into the brain. The experience is sometimes fatal, often devastating, but never painful. Surprisingly, our human brains are not supplied with pain receptors!

The medical term for a brain attack is stroke and most people are conscious when it happens. Loss of consciousness may result in a minority of serious cases and many strokes take place when the individual is sleeping. The majority of patients, although dazed and confused, can vividly recall the onset of stroke. Even now, twenty-three years after the event, I can remember every last detail...

It had been a glorious summer's day in August. Enjoying the solitude and tranquillity of my own company, I had taken a leisurely stroll in the woods before stopping for lunch. Just after ten o'clock that evening, as I sat alone in my study at home preparing my workload for Monday, I reached forward for a glass of water on my desk, spilling it all over my paperwork.

Not entirely at once, but gradually, in terrifying waves of panic, I became aware that part of one side of my body was paralysed. I could barely move or control my quivering lips, from which saliva was escaping. The two sides of my mouth were shuddering involuntarily but not in harmony: one side was more sluggish than the other. I couldn't understand why, according to the clock facing me, half an hour seemed to have elapsed in the time it had taken me to mop up the spillage with my handkerchief.

The right half of my body felt numb and heavy and my face didn't seem to fit any more. It occurred to me that maybe I should call a doctor but then, I wondered, if I went to bed, perhaps I would be all right in the morning.

EXPRESS RECOVERY TIP
Don't make an appointment to visit your doctor. Call an ambulance immediately.

When, as if in a dream, or rather a nightmare, I probed myself disbelievingly with a finger that worked, I discovered that one corner of my mouth was an inch higher than the other. I cursed and swore, or rather I tried to, but all that would come out was gibberish! It dawned on me that I was living a nightmare, not dreaming it.

Original screenplay by
©David M Hinds

TASER

Taser

an original multi-award-winning screenplay:

a darkly comedic psychosexual thriller by

David M Hinds

WGA Registration Number: 2128360

Phone: 01752 601956 (Inside UK)
Phone: 01144 1752601956 (From USA)
Email: david@davidmhinds.com
Website: davidmhinds.com

Library of Congress United States
Copyright Registration: PAu 4-098-739
Copyright Witness (UK) Reg: 284691426

David M Hinds International Film Festival Screenplay Awards

SCREENPLAY AWARDS _OUTRIGHT WINS_ FOR "TASER":

Oniros Film Awards New York	**WINNER – BEST THRILLER SCRIPT**	Dec. 2021
WorldFest Houston	**PLATINUM WINNER – BEST THRILLER**	2022
Golden Sparrow International Film Festival	**WINNER - BEST FEATURE SCRIPT/SCREENPLAY**	May 2022
Košice International Film Festival	**WINNER – BEST THRILLER SCREENPLAY**	May 2022
Prague International Film Awards	**WINNER – BEST ACTION SCREENPLAY**	Spring 2022
Stanley Film Awards	**WINNER – BEST FEATURE SCRIPT**	June 2022
International Manhattan Film Awards	**WINNER – BEST COMEDY**	2022

SCREENPLAY AWARDS _OUTRIGHT WINS_ FOR TASER'S ALTERNATE TITLE: "THE HAPPINESS ANGEL":

Oniros Film Awards New York	**WINNER – BEST ORIGINAL SCRIPT**	April 2022
Oniros Film Awards New York	**WINNER – BEST THRILLER SCRIPT**	April 2022
Oniros Film Awards New York	**WINNER – BEST 1ST TIME SCREENWRITER – FEATURE**	April 2022
Golden Eagle Film Festival India	**WINNER - BEST FEATURE SCRIPT / SCREENPLAY**	May 2022
8 & HalFilm Fellini Festival Italy	**WINNER - BEST INTERNATIONAL FEATURE SCRIPT**	June 2022
Sweet Democracy Film Awards	**WINNER – BEST FEATURE SCRIPT**	June 2022
Florence Film Awards	**SILVER WINNER - BEST FEATURE SCRIPT**	June 2022
New York Movie Awards	**WINNER – BEST FEATURE SCRIPT**	June 2022
WorldFest Houston	**SILVER WINNER – BEST COMEDY**	2022

INT. FUNCTION ROOM, SAVOY HOTEL, LONDON - NIGHT

CANDY TOWNE, mid-twenties, possessing the kind of forced positivity that comes from a dark past, with a spark in her eyes that hints of wildness, is **LIVE VLOGGING** through the lens of her iPhone 13 Pro Max.

> CANDY
> Hi Honeys. Happiness is honesty.
> So I'll be honest with you. Winning
> this award tonight would make me
> truly ecstatic!

Candy spins the camera to reveal she's recording herself at a packed awards ceremony.

> CANDY (CONT'D)
> I know - very unhealthy. A trophy
> is just a piece of metal and I
> shouldn't let my self-worth be
> dictated by the approval of others.

In the background, JASON WOOD, authoritative, suave, late-thirties, and dressed in Savile Row black, mounts the stage.

> CANDY (CONT'D)
> But sometimes you just gotta give
> yourself a break and enjoy it for
> what it is.

Candy pauses as Jason starts talking, keeping him in the background of the shot.

> JASON
> I'm here to do one thing only, so
> without further ado, the award for
> the LAMBOURN COURT INTERNATIONAL
> Stress Management Practitioner of
> the Year 2022 goes to...

Candy theatrically crosses her fingers for the camera.

Jason opens the envelope and reads out the winner.

> JASON (CONT'D)
> Candy Towne. A brilliant therapist
> whom I greatly respect and admire,
> known to millions of YouTubers as
> *THE HAPPINESS ANGEL*.

Candy's smile dazzles with delight.

EXT. PANORAMIC VIEW OF INNERMOST LONDON (UK) - DAY

A rumble of thunder sounds. Lightning streaks across a bright late-February morning sky.

In a spectacular firework finale, a cloud-to-ground thunderbolt strikes the iron railings to the balcony of a corner penthouse in Rathbone Square, Fitzrovia - a haven of calm tucked between Charlotte Street and Soho.

EXT. CORNER PENTHOUSE IN RATHBONE SQUARE - CONT.

Glimpsed through the master bedroom's French windows, two startled individuals are caught in its sudden *flash*: Candy Towne and Jason Wood.

Her toned muscles flex as she strains for a better view. He's sombre, dressed all in black again, and walks away.

INT. PENTHOUSE - MOMENTS LATER

OVER THE CLOSED MASTER BEDROOM DOOR

                    FEMALE SCREAM
          Bastard!

A thud is heard. A gasp, and then the door *SHAKES*.

An early title card reads: "Inspired by true events."

PULL BACK TO REVEAL

A bookcase stacked with psychology titles. Prominent is a set of four large Lambourn Court International (LCI) stress management training manuals authored by Jason Wood.

Below, on a coffee table, is a well-thumbed copy of this morning's (Saturday, February 26th, 2022) newspaper, open at the Business Franchising pages.

A double-page spread features last night's LCI Practitioner of the Year Awards at The Savoy Hotel. Pictured is a smiling Candy Towne being presented with the winner's trophy by LCI founder and chief executive Jason Wood.

The door bursts open. Jason appears. *WHACK!* He's hit on the back of his head by a book hurled from inside the room. He turns...

MASTER BEDROOM

Candy Towne, by the French windows, prepares to leap.

                    CANDY
          I'll fucking make you love me if
          it kills me.

Jason, nursing his head between his hands, is shocked to see Candy leap, fully dressed, in one aesthetically perfect manoeuvre, onto his king-size, antique iron bed with brass rings and bed knobs.

She lands upright on the bedspread and glares down at him.

                    JASON
          Get off.

                    CANDY
          If you want to get off with me, do
          the gallant thing, get on with it.

From her vantage point five feet seven inches above the
top of the bed, Candy spots something that strikes her as
bizarre behind the chaise longue.

                    CANDY (CONT'D)
          What's that?

She points her finger at it.

A pair of handcuffs is revealed attached to a chain.

But Jason's eyes do not follow her finger...

His gaze lowers, and the air beneath him freezes as his
eyes lock onto the missile that rebounded from the back of
his head and landed on its 413-year-old cover open at the
page where he had handwritten the words: *To Lady Helen of
Shrewsbury, I will love you forever - Jason xxx.*

He grasps the cloth-covered book by its spine (faded over
the centuries from its original brown colour to gunmetal
grey), and sinks to his knees.

                    JASON
          Helen, I'm so sorry...

He kisses the cover and fires a look at Candy so fierce,
she sits.

He then rises to his feet, inspects with reverence the
brownish-cream pages of the ancient book of poems for
damage, and advances, book in hand, towards Candy.

                    JASON (CONT'D)
               (in a measured tone)
          This is not the assault weapon of
          choice. It is a rare 1609 edition
          of Shakespeare's Sonnets; only
          thirteen exist today.

                    CANDY
          Who's Lady Helen of Shrewsbury?

Jason swallows. The muscles in his jaw tense.

                    JASON
          Get out.

Candy, non-compliant but calmer, canoodles up to him. In
a low-pitched voice, she states the obvious...

                        CANDY
            You're emotionally frozen in time.
            You need defrosting.

She places the palm of her hand on the sensitive area of
his trousers. He's aroused, but he brushes her hand aside.

                        JASON
            I know your inner secrets. It
            would be unethical... *I can't.*

                        CANDY
            You sanctimonious pussycat. That
            was five years ago. You've got a
            ghost in your past. Unload on me.

                        JASON
            You were invited this morning for
            a gratulatory brunch, not therapy!

                        CANDY
            I want to know your secret.

                        JASON
                  (looking daggers)
            You earned your award on sheer
            merit. Don't fuck with me.

                        CANDY
            I know that. *How dare you?*

She slaps him hard and fast across the face.

The stinging imprint of her hand reddens his cheek.

                        CANDY (CONT'D)
                  (backing off, aghast)
            Sorry. I didn't mean to.

                        JASON
            Get out. Or I will disenfranchise
            you.

                        CANDY
            You can't. You wouldn't! I was
            your first...

Jason glances menacingly at his watch.

                        JASON
            Try me. You've got ten seconds to
            save your career.

Candy meets his pitiless gaze. She grabs her handbag and
gets the hell out of there. The front door gets it. *SLAM!*

DISSOLVE TO

EXT. THE A38 TRUNK ROAD TO THE SOUTH-WEST - DAY

Amid the dense, bumper-to-bumper, slow-moving traffic is
Candy driving her blue electric Mini Cooper S with a light
blue multitone roof.

To the astonishment of the MIDDLE-AGED MALE DRIVER of a
Mercedes right behind the Mini, Candy - emergency lights
flashing - makes a skilful, saucy and downright illegal
six-point turn to escape the hold-up.

INT. RED MERCEDES SALOON CAR - CONT.

Two teenagers - A BOY AND A GIRL - sit in the rear seats.
They are engrossed in a YouTube clip on an iPad.

                    CANDY
               (on video)
          There are many steps to happiness,
          but the starting point is to accept
          yourself for who you are. Avoid
          the trap of craving approval from -

                    TEENAGE BOY
          Wow, that Happiness Angel's cute.

                    TEENAGE GIRL
          Shush! I want to hear her -

                    FATHER AT THE WHEEL
               (to his wife opposite)
          Look! The audacity of the girl -

The boy glances up just as Candy's Mini shoots off across
oncoming traffic and into a narrow single-track road
signposted to Dartmoor.

                    TEENAGE BOY
          It's her... The famous one - *The
          Happiness Angel!*

He snatches the iPad to show his Dad.

WHITE VAN MAN blasts his horn at Candy as she completes
the final stage of her manoeuvre across his path.

EXT. PANORAMIC VISTA OF DARTMOOR - MID-AFTERNOON

Rolling moorland and ancient granite tors abound. Ponies
roam, streams sparkle, and crows and ravens fly overhead.

We zone in on Candy's Mini parked in an isolated moss-
covered beauty spot with sheep grazing by a narrow road.

There is a black Alfa Romeo parked ahead, but we do not
focus on that, although we are aware of its existence.

INT. MINI - CONTINUOUS

Candy applies fresh make-up as she sits in the driver's
seat. She then talks to the lens of the camera on her
iPhone as she videos her regular happiness vlog.

The iPhone is coupled to a mini-tripod on the dashboard
and angled so that YouTube viewers will see Candy centred
in the frame with the tranquil backdrop of Dartmoor through
the rear window. The sliding sunroof is WIDE OPEN. She's
part-way through her performance.

>   CANDY
>   Happiness is within our grasp, but
>   sometimes just out of reach. I
>   can't fake it with you guys. The
>   truth is I'm in love with Mr Right,
>   but he's not in love with me. I
>   can never be truly happy until -

Her eyes stray from the lens, veering left of centre.

>   CANDY (CONT'D)
>   - he falls in love with me, or I
>   stop loving him...

Her mouth gapes in horror. Her eyes widen in disbelief as
they travel from left to right across the windscreen.

>   CANDY (CONT'D)
>   *Jesus Christ!*

A scruffy-looking GUY, tall and mean-mouthed, in faded
denims drifts into her line of vision.

He's hauling behind him by her curly red hair, a gaunt
young WOMAN in her early-twenties with sallow, sunken cheeks
and piercing, deep-set eyes. She struggles to break free
of her captor.

>   THE HOSTAGE
>   (wailing)
>   You're hurting me.

The KIDNAPPER wrenches open the passenger door of the Alfa,
throws her inside, and slams the door shut. He darts to
the other side and jumps in.

Before roaring off, wheels spinning, with a noisy Italianate
howl, he reverses into the Mini. ***BANG!***

The impact sends the tripod complete with iPhone flying.
Instinctively, Candy's hands shoot up to shield her face,
propelling it upwards, and the whole paraphernalia goes
straight out through the open sunroof.

>   CANDY
>   You evil bastard!

She jabs the START button and races in pursuit, stabbing the SMARTNAV control button as she accelerates to 37mph in 3.9 seconds in absolute silence.

A pony ambles into the road... She slams on the brakes and swerves, *Go-Cart-style*, to avoid it.

> SMARTNAV OPERATOR (V.O.)
> (dialling tone rings)
> Hello, Candy. My name's Jane.
> (Liverpool accent)
> Where are you travelling to today?

> CANDY
> Don't need a route. This is an emergency. Please call the police and patch them into my satellite navigation system.

> SMARTNAV OPERATOR (V.O.)
> Have you had an accident? Do you require help?

> CANDY
> I've witnessed a kidnapping. I'm chasing the getaway car. A black Alfa Romeo.

> SMARTNAV OPERATOR (V.O.)
> Registration number?

> CANDY
> Don't know yet.

> SMARTNAV OPERATOR (V.O.)
> OK, Candy, I've got your location in the Dartmoor National Park. I'm contacting the Devon and Cornwall Constabulary as we speak.

SERIES OF HIGH-SPEED CHASE SCENES ACROSS DARTMOOR

- Mini weaves in and out of bends, near-miss overtaking.

- *Shudders* over a teeth-shattering cattle grid.

- Mini closes in on the Alfa. Tailgates it.

- Alfa swerves left. Mini overshoots. Backs-up. Turns.

- Candy curses. *She's lost sight of the Alfa!*

Candy speeds up, rounds a downhill bend, and there, at the end of the track, by an impassable river and a ramshackle cottage, is the kidnapper's car.

He jumps out... Candy jams on the brakes and stops short.

INT. RIVERSIDE APPROACH - DAY

                    SMARTNAV OPERATOR (V.O.) (CONT'D)
          Candy, a message has come in from
          the Devon and Cornwall Constabulary -

                    CANDY
          Thank God! Are they nearly here?

                    SMARTNAV OPERATOR (V.O.)
          They're warning you not to exceed
          the speed limit or endanger other
          road users, or you could be liable
          to prosecution under the Road
          Traffic Act 1988.

                    CANDY
          What?

The kidnapper, meanwhile, sneaks up on Candy. He grabs
her by the hair through the panoramic sunroof and wrenches
her head up as far as the seat belt will allow. Her throat
is constricted by the roof edge. She can't scream...

                    THE KIDNAPPER
               (his mouth inches
                from her eyes)
          Don't need you, bitch. Fuck off.

With the air of a man without a care in the world, he lets
go of her and struts off back towards the Alfa.

Candy collapses back into the car seat, stunned. Her foot
lands hard on the accelerator, driving it flat to the floor.

The Mini lurches silently forward. The kidnapper TURNS.
Too late! She's doing fifty and hits him. **WHAM!**

Through the windscreen and, a split-second later, through
the sunroof, we see the kidnapper fold and crumple as he
catapults over the bonnet and roof. Bones CRACK as he
lands head first with a bang and a deathly rumble on the
rigid back end of the roof.

Candy's eyes dart up and backwards to the source of the
sound. There is an indent to the roof lining in the shape
of an inverted human skull. Blood oozes through the open
roof. A drop lands on her lip. By reflex, she licks it.

She shudders and jerks her head forward. The RIVER DART
is *dead ahead!* Deep in the footwell, Candy's foot fumbles
for the brake pedal. *Misses!* She freezes with fear.

EXT. RIVERBANK - CONTINUOUS

The Mini's wheels lose contact with the ground as the car
becomes airborne. The car swirls around in a slow waltz,
before it crash-lands on water.

INT. MINI - CONTINUOUS

Airbags burst into life around Candy. Cold, dank water
rises above her ankles and then her knees. She gropes for
her seat belt buckle, releases it, and makes a grab for
the door handle. *It won't release.*

Her fingers slither off the handle, exhausted.

>   SMARTNAV OPERATOR (V.O.)
>   Candy, have the police arrived?

>   CANDY
>   No, I'm bloody drowning all alone.

Reinvigorated, Candy clambers onto the car seat and hauls
herself up through the sunroof. She squeezes out.

>   SMARTNAV OPERATOR (V.O.)
>   Talk to me. Candy... Talk to me.

EXT. IN THE RIVER - CONTINUOUS

The ghost of the Smartnav operator's voice gurgles and
grounds with the Mini as Candy wade-swims to dry land.

EXT. RIVERBANK - CONTINUOUS

Candy drags herself, muddy, exhausted and sodden, up onto
the bank. Her wet clothes leave little to the imagination.

She sits for a moment, then totters towards the Alfa in
search of the hostage. *She's not there!* Candy's eyes
scan the vicinity. She spots her peeping out from behind
the cottage, clutching a garden spade in weapon mode.

>   THE HOSTAGE
>   Don't you come near me, you raving
>   psycho. You've just killed my
>   husband.

Candy freezes, stung by her words. In the distance, sirens
sound as emergency vehicles draw ever closer.

>   CANDY
>   But... He kidnapped you. He dragged
>   you into the car. *I saw it!*

>   THE HOSTAGE
>   It's a sex game.

>   CANDY
>   (incredulous)
>   A game! How dare you? *Why?*

>   THE HOSTAGE
>   'Cos it turns him on. That's kinda
>   the point.

                    CANDY
                (indignantly)
        He REVERSED into me.

                    THE HOSTAGE
        Car's new. He didn't mean to.

                    CANDY
        But he brought you here?

                    THE HOSTAGE
                (shrieking)
        We fucking live here!

The sound of sirens grows louder. A convoy of police cars
and ambulances arrive. The hostage drops the spade. The
OCCUPANTS of the first patrol car spring out. Candy, jaw
set, adrenalin racing, squelches towards them.

                    THE HOSTAGE (CONT'D)
                (pointing at Candy)
        She murdered my husband. *I saw it!*

                    FIRST POLICEMAN
                (to Candy)
        Stop. Hands up. Stand still.

Candy, wet, indignant and dishevelled, staggers towards
the nearest policeman to protest her innocence... But
then she slips on the mossy surface and slides out of
control towards him. He draws his Taser and takes aim.

                    FIRST POLICEMAN (CONT'D)
                (before firing)
        Stop, or I fire.

In a flash, two long copper wires shoot out from the main
unit of the Taser gun to their points of contact on Candy's
body. The projectiles stay connected to the Taser gun.

One strikes Candy on the fleshy frontal part of her neck,
the other penetrates her blouse and left nipple. She
stiffens and then writhes in convolutions of agony as
electrical pulses surge through her.

She rocks backwards as though she's taken an almighty THUMP -
but then, *after the initial shockwave* - the reverberations
make her pitch back and forth, ever closer to the policeman.

The 'hostage' looks on in astonishment mingled with delight.

Despite a 50,000-VOLT TASER DOUBLE HIT, Candy stays upright
for 17 SECONDS like a dancing marionette jerked to the
pulse of electrons and protons! Until the Taser stops...
Then she collapses to the ground at the feet of the first
police officer.

FADE TO BLACK

Lightning Source UK Ltd.
Milton Keynes UK
UKHW051942290822
408042UK00015B/246

WILLIAM SHAKESPEARE'S

HAMLET

CAMPFIRE®

KALYANI NAVYUG MEDIA PVT LTD

C000139325

WILLIAM SHAKESPEARE'S

HAMLET

Adapted by
Malini Roy
Illustrated by
Naresh Kumar
Colored by
Ashwani Kashyap & Vijay Sharma
Cover Art & Design
Naresh Kumar & Vijay Sharma

CAMPFIRE®
www.campfire.co.in

Mission Statement

To entertain and educate young minds by creating unique illustrated books
that recount stories of human values, arouse curiosity in the world around us,
and inspire with tales of great deeds of unforgettable people.

Published by Kalyani Navyug Media Pvt Ltd
101 C, Shiv House, Hari Nagar Ashram, New Delhi 110014, India
ISBN: 978-93-81182-51-2

Copyright © 2019 Kalyani Navyug Media Pvt Ltd

All rights reserved. Published by Campfire, an imprint of Kalyani Navyug Media Pvt Ltd.

No part of this publication may be reproduced, stored in a retrieval system, or transmitted in
any form or by any means, electronic, mechanical, photocopying, recording, or otherwise

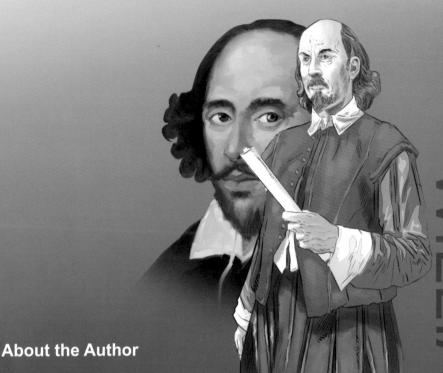

WILLIAM SHAKESPEARE

About the Author

Famously known as 'The Bard of Avon', William Shakespeare was born in Stratford-upon-Avon, most probably on April 23, 1564. We say probably because till date, nobody has conclusive evidence for Shakespeare's birthday.

His father, John Shakespeare, was a successful local businessman and his mother, Mary Arden, was the daughter of a wealthy landowner. In 1582, an eighteen-year-old William married an older woman named Anne Hathaway. Soon, they had their first daughter, Susanna and later, another two children. William's only son, Hamnet, died at the tender age of eleven.

Translated into innumerable languages across the globe, Shakespeare's plays and sonnets are undoubtedly the most studied writings in the English language. A rare playwright, he excelled in tragedies, comedies, and histories. Skillfully combining entertainment with unmatched poetry, some of his most famous plays are Othello, Macbeth, A Midsummer Night's Dream, Romeo and Juliet, and The Merchant of Venice, among many others.

Shakespeare was also an actor. In 1599, he became one of the partners in the new Globe Theatre in London and a part owner of his own theater company called 'The Chamberlain's Men'—a group of remarkable actors who were also business partners and close friends of Shakespeare. When Queen Elizabeth died in 1603 and was succeeded by her cousin King James of Scotland, 'The Chamberlain's Men' was renamed 'The King's Men'.

Shakespeare died in 1616. It is not clear how he died although his vicar suggested it was from heavy drinking.

The characters he created and the stories he told have held the interest of people for the past 400 years! Till date, his plays are performed all over the world and have been turned into movies, comics, cartoons

Claudius
Present King of Denmark
Hamlet's Uncle

Gertrude
Queen of Denmark
Hamlet's Mother

King Hamlet
The Late King of Denmark
Hamlet's Father

Polonius
Chief Counsellor
to the King

Hamlet
Prince of Denmark

Ophelia
Polonius's Daughter

Laertes
Polonius's Son

Elsinore, Denmark.

Has this thing appeared again tonight?

I have seen nothing.

And you won't! There are no such things as ghosts. You're like scared children, the pair of you.

We've both seen it, Horatio. I swear, it's the spirit of our dead king.

Rubbish!

Look, it comes again!

Look, Horatio! It is the King!

'Tis gone!

It wanted to speak, but then the cock crew, calling it back to the tomb.

We must tell young Hamlet, the dead king's son, what we have seen this night. Upon my life, the spirit will speak to him.

Let's do it! I know where we can find him.

Why, that is a loving and a fair reply, Hamlet. Come Gertrude, we shall drink to this tonight. Denmark shall be merry.

O God! A beast would have mourned longer. Married to my uncle and my father within a month. It cannot come to good.

Hail to your lordship.

I am glad to see you well, Horatio. What brings you here from Wittenberg?

The family home of Polonius, Principal Secretary of State.

Before I leave, Ophelia, I need you to listen to me. Don't let Hamlet break your heart. His love may be sweet, but it won't last. The perfume and suppliance of a minute, no more.

No more but so?

His greatness weighed, his will is not his own. He is a prince. He may not be free to marry the one he loves, as unvalued persons do. On his choice depends the sanctity and health of his whole state.

My good brother, do not as some ungracious pastors do, show me the steep and thorny way to heaven, while like a puffed and reckless libertine you yourself tread the primrose path of dalliance.

Oh fear me not. I stay too long—but here my Father comes.

13

Laertes, hurry up, your ship leaves soon!

Take my blessings, and remember my words in France. Give every man thy ear, but few thy voice. Neither a borrower nor a lender be; for loan oft loses both itself and friend.

This above all: to thine ownself be true, and it must follow, as the night the day, thou canst not then be false to any man.

Most humbly I take my leave, my lord.

Farewell Ophelia, and remember well what I have said to you.

It is locked in my memory.

What did Laertes say to you, Ophelia?

Something about Lord Hamlet, Father.

What is between you? Give me up the truth.

He has of late made many tenders of his affection to me.

Affection? Pooh! You speak like a green girl. Do not sell yourself so cheaply! From this time forth you are not to see him or speak with him.

I... I shall obey, my lord.

God be with you, farewell.

Farewell, my lord.

Ophelia! What is the matter?

Oh my lord, my lord, I have been so affrighted!

My lord, as I was sewing in my closet, Lord Hamlet came in.

His face was pale as his shirt. He was trembling and looked as if he had escaped from Hell.

Mad for your love? What did he say?

With one hand he gripped my wrist, and clapped the other to his forehead. He stayed like that for a long time. Then he sighed and walked out of the room.

Have you been unkind to him lately?

No, my good lord. I only refused to see him or answer his letters, as you commanded.

I had feared that his love for you was not genuine, but perhaps I was wrong.

Come, we must tell the King.

Elsinore Palace.

Welcome, dear Rosencrantz and Guildenstern! You are aware that Hamlet has been behaving strangely of late. Perhaps as his childhood friends, you could find out what troubles him.

Your efforts shall receive such appreciation as fits a King's remembrance.

Your wish is our command.

We lay our service freely at your feet to be commanded.

I beseech you to visit my son without delay.

As you command, your Majesty.

What do you read, my lord?

Words, words, words.

What is the matter that you read, my lord?

Slanders sir, for the satirical rogue says here that old men have a plentiful lack of wit. Which sir, though I most powerfully and potently believe, yet I hold it not honesty to have it thus set down. For yourself sir shall grow old as I am, if like a crab you could go backward.

Though this be madness, yet there is method in it. How pregnant sometimes his replies are! I will leave him, and subtly contrive the means of meeting between him and my daughter.

My honourable lord, I will most humbly take leave of you.

You cannot, sir, take from me anything that I will more willingly part withal—except my life, except my life, except my life.

Welcome, good friends. We'll watch a play tomorrow. Can you play 'The Murder of Gonzago'?

Yes, my lord.

Very well. My good friends, I'll leave you till night.

O is it not monstrous that this player here, but in a fiction, in a dream of passion, could force his soul so to his own conceit? What is Hecuba to him, or he to Hecuba, that he should weep for her? What would he do, had he the motive and the cue for passion that I have? Am I a coward? But I am pigeon-livered, and lack gall to make oppression bitter. Bloody, bawdy villain! Remorseless, treacherous, lecherous, kindless villain! Oh, vengeance!

I have heard that guilty creatures sitting at a play have by the very cunning of the scene been struck to the soul. I shall have these players play something like the murder of my Father before mine uncle. I will observe his looks. If he but blench, I know my course. The spirit that I have seen perhaps, out of my weakness and my melancholy, abuses me to damn me. I will have grounds more relative than this. The play is the thing wherein I'll catch the conscience of the King.

Sweet Gertrude, leave us too, for we have arranged it such that Hamlet may come here, and, as if by accident, meet Ophelia. Her father and I shall remain unseen and watch the encounter, in order to frankly judge whether Hamlet suffers from the affliction of love.

Ophelia, I do wish that your beauty and goodness are the happy cause of Hamlet's wildness. I hope your virtues will bring him to his wonted way again, to both your honours.

Madam, I wish it may.

Ophelia, walk this way. Read this book, so that the show of such an exercise may colour your loneliness.

I hear him coming. Let us withdraw, my lord.

To be or not to be, that is the question. Whether 'tis nobler in the mind to suffer the slings and arrows of outrageous fortune, or to take arms against a sea of troubles, and by opposing end them. To die, to sleep—no more. And by a sleep to say we end the heart-ache and the thousand natural shocks that flesh is heir to—it is a consummation devoutly to be wished. To die, to sleep—to sleep, perchance to dream.

Ay, there's the rub. For in that sleep of death what dreams may come, when we have shuffled off this mortal coil, must give us pause. For who would bear the whips and scorns of time, the oppressor's wrong, the proud man's contumely, when he himself might his quietus make with a bare bodkin?

But that the dread of something after death, the undiscovered country from whose bourn no traveller returns, puzzles the will. And makes us rather bear those ills we have, than fly to others we know not of. Thus conscience does make cowards of us all, and enterprises of great pitch and moment lose the name of action.

Soft you now, the fair Ophelia.

My lord, I have remembrances of yours that I have longed long to re-deliver. I pray you now receive them.

No, I never gave you aught.

My honoured lord, you know right well you d and with them words of sweet breath composed made the things more ri Their perfume lost, tak these again. Rich gifts w poor when givers prov unkind.

Ha, ha, are you honest?

My lord?

Are you fair?

What means your lordship?

32

Act 3   Scene 2

Later in the day, Hamlet watches the actors prepare for the play.

Do not saw the air too much with your hand thus; use your limbs gently. Nor is there a need to be too tame. Let your own discretion be your tutor. Suit the action to the word and the word to the action, with this special observance that you do not overstep the modesty of nature. Anything so overdone defeats the purpose of acting, whose end is to hold the mirror up to nature.

What news do you bring, my lord? Will the King see this piece of work?

Yes, and the Queen will see it too. They will be here shortly.

Horatio, tonight, a play will be performed before the King. One scene will replay my Father's death as the ghost described it to me. When this scene is played out, watch my uncle. If he has a guilty conscience, his face will give him away.

36

How fares our cousin Hamlet?

Excellent in faith.

Come here, my dear Hamlet, sit by me.

No good Mother, here is metal more attractive.

You are merry, my lord.

What should a man do but be merry? For look you how cheerfully my Mother looks, and my Father has died within two hours.

No, it is twice two months, my lord.

So long? O heavens! Die two months ago, and not forgotten yet?

39

In Queen Gertrude's hamber, Polonius prepares to carry out his plan.

Tell him that enough is enough and you have run out of patience for his pranks. I will hide in here and listen.

I assure you, I shall handle this well. Withdraw, I hear him coming.

Mother, Mother, Mother!

Now Mother, what is the matter?

Hamlet, thou hast thy Father much offended.

Mother, you have my Father much offended.

Come, come, you answer with an idle tongue. Have you forgot me?

Not so. You are the Queen, your husband's brother's wife. And would it were not so, you are my Mother.

Enough!

Come, come, sit down. You shall not budge.

As killing a King?

Yes lady, that was my word. Stop wringing your hands. Peace! Sit down and let me wring your heart, for so I shall. Look here upon this picture, and on this.

See what a grace was seated on this brow. An eye like Mars, to threaten and command. A combination and a form indeed, where every god did seem to set his seal to give the world assurance of a man. This was your husband.

Here is your husband, like a mildewed ear blasting his wholesome brother. Have you eyes? You cannot call it love, for at your age the heyday in the blood is tame, it is humble, and waits upon the judgement. And what judgement would step from this to this?

O Hamlet, speak no more. You turn my eyes into my very soul.

A murderer and a villain, a cutpurse of the empire and rule, that from a shelf the precious diadem stole and put it in his pocket!

Oh speak to me no more. These words like daggers enter in my ears. No more, sweet Hamlet.

You heavenly guards! What would your gracious figure?

Alas, he is mad!

Do you not come your tardy son to chide, that lapsed in time and passion lets go by the important acting of your dread command? Oh say!

Look, amazement on thy Mother sits. Speak to her, Hamlet.

How is it with you lady?

Alas, how is it with you my son, that you speak with the air? What are you looking at?

Look you, how pale he glares. Do you see nothing there?

No, nothing.

He is leaving us.

Confess yourself to heaven. Repent what is past, avoid what is to come. Good night—but go not to my uncle's bed. I must be cruel only to be kind. One word more, good lady.

If the bloat King tempts you to bed again, and tries to make you speak the truth about me, do not tell him that I am essentially not in madness, but mad in craft.

If words be made of breath, and breath of life, I have no life to breathe what you have said to me.

I must go to England, do you know that? The letters are sealed, and my two schoolfellows, whom I will trust as I will trust fanged snakes, bear the mandate.

Good night, Mother.

seems unlikely that Hamlet's departure will be taken well by the public. But such a grave disease as this can only be cured by a tough measure, or not at all.

My lord, we could not make him tell us where he has hid the body.

But where is he?

Outside, my lord. Guarded, and ready to be summoned by you.

Bring him before us.

Now Hamlet, where is Polonius?

At supper.

Not where he eats, but where he is eaten. A certain convocation of politic worms are nibbling at him.

What do you mean by this? Where is Polonius?

In heaven, send for him there. If your messenger find him not there, seek him in the other place yourself.

Near the castle of Elsinore.

Go captain, offer my greetings to the Danish king. Tell him that by his licence, Fortinbras asks for the passage of his army through his kingdom, as promised.

Yes, my lord.

Good sir, whose forces are these? Who commands them, sir? Where are they headed?

The King of Norway, sir. His nephew Fortinbras commands us. We are off to attack Poland.

The army charges against the main of Poland, sir, or for some frontier?

To speak the truth, we stand to gain only a small patch of land that has no profit in it, only the name. The soil is so fallow that I would not pay five ducats to farm it.

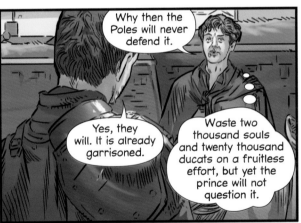

Why then the Poles will never defend it.

Yes, they will. It is already garrisoned.

Waste two thousand souls and twenty thousand ducats on a fruitless effort, but yet the prince will not question it.

Wealth and peace has wrongly convinced him; he is dead inside, and yet, on the outside, no one can see what caused his malady.

I humbly thank you, sir.

God be with you, sir.

Shall we go, my lord?

How all occasions do inform against me, and spur my dull revenge!

Oh, from this time forth, my thoughts be bloody or be nothing worth.

Save yourself, my lord. Young Laertes has come to your gate with an angry crowd. Your officers fail to hold him. And the crowd cry 'Laertes shall be King.'

O you vile King, give me back my Father!

Calm down, good Laertes.

What is the cause, Laertes, that your rebellion is so massive?

Where is my Father?

Dead.

But not by him.

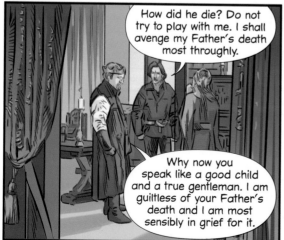

How did he die? Do not try to play with me. I shall avenge my Father's death most throughly.

Why now you speak like a good child and a true gentleman. I am guiltless of your Father's death and I am most sensibly in grief for it.

Let her come in!

What noise is that?

56

Laertes, I am one with you in grief. If you wish, go and discuss this matter with your wisest friends. Let them judge if I had been just with your Father. If you still doubt my honesty, I will happily give up my crown, my life, and everything else I call mine to you.

His cause of death has been concealed. There was no noble rite, nor formal ostentation. I must call these things in question. I must know why everything was done secretly.

So you shall.

And where the offence is, let the great axe fall. I pray you come with me.

Two months since you were gone, a gentleman of Normandy came here. He knew you. The French are generally good horsemen, but this gallant man could create magic on horseback.

Upon my life, he must be Lamord.

It was him. He spoke very highly of your talent at fencing, Laertes. Praising your art with the rapier, he said that it would be a sight indeed if one could match you. Since Hamlet heard this, he kept wishing you would come back soon, so that he could invite you to a friendly match. You know how keen he is on this sport.

Hamlet, when he returns, shall know you have come home. We will put on those who shall praise your excellence. Therefore, you may invite Hamlet to a friendly match, and he will not refuse.

Hamlet being most generous, and free from all contriving, will not examine the foils. With ease, or a little shuffling, you may choose a sword without difficulty. So, in this match, you will get a chance to avenge your father's death.

My Queen!

One woe doth tread upon another's heel. Your sister has drowned, Laertes.

Drowned! Oh, where?

There is a willow grows aslant a brook. There with fantastic garlands did she make. On the pendant boughs her weeds clambering to hang, an envious sliver broke, when down her weedy trophies and herself fell in the weeping brook. Her clothes spread wide, and mermaid-like awhile they bore her up, which time she chanted snatches of old lauds...

'But long it could not be till that her garments, heavy with their drink, pulled the poor wretch from her melodious lay to muddy death.'

Too much of water you have, poor Ophelia. Therefore I forbid my tears. Adieu, my lord.

Let us follow him, Gertrude. How much I had to do to calm his rage! Now I fear this incident will upset him again. Therefore, let us follow.

68

69

This is mere madness.

What is the reason that you treat me like this? I loved you ever—but it is no matter. Let Hercules himself do what he may, the cat will mew, and dog will have his day.

Good Horatio, please be with Hamlet. Gertrude, set some watch over your son. This grave shall have a living monument.

Strengthen your patience. Remember our last night's conversation?

This letter contains proof of Claudius and his evil intentions.

On my first night away, I could not sleep. I got up in the night and went to the cabin of Rosencrantz and Guildenstern.

There I found a sealed packet, and stole it. Then I withdrew to my own ro to unseal their grand commission. M fears made me forget my manners. found, Horatio—O royal knavery!—an e command, larded with several charg against me, importing Denmark's hea and England's too, that without dela my head should be struck off.

'I found myself trapped by villainies. So I sat down to write a new commission. I wrote it as an earnest appeal from the King, as England was his faithful tributary, that the bearers of the letter should be put to sudden death.'

'I had my father's signet in my purse, which was the model of that Danish seal. I folded up the letter neatly, placed it in the envelope, and sealed it, to make it look exactly like the original one. Then I kept it where the original letter was. No one would know the difference. The next day we had our sea-fight, and you are aware of what happened after that.'

So Guildenstern and Rosencrantz must pay for it.

It was their choice to spy on me. Their death is not on my conscience.

Why, what a King is this!

He has killed my Father, the King, and made my Mother cheap. He has stolen the throne that was mine by right, and tried to take my life too. Is it not perfect conscience to stop him before he can do more evil?

What happened in England shall be known to the King soon enough.

Yes, soon enough. But the interim is mine. I am very sorry, that I behaved badly with Laertes. He is fighting for his father, and so am I. I shall court his favours.

Welcome back to Denmark, your lordship. If your lordship were at leisure, I should impart a thing to you from his Majesty.

I will receive it sir, with all diligence of spirit. Put your bonnet to its right use. It is for the head.

I thank your lordship, it is very hot. His Majesty bade me signify to you that he has laid a great wager on your head. Sir, this is the matter—

Sir, here is newly come to court Laertes; believe me an absolute gentleman, full of most excellent differences, of very soft society and great showing. You are not ignorant of what excellence Laertes is. I mean sir for his weapon; rapier and dagger. The King has laid that in a dozen passes between yourself and him, he shall not exceed you three hits.

Yes, I know one cannot possibly count all his perfections. But sir, why do you take his name? What is this about?

The King sir has wagered with him six Barbary horses, against which he has impawned six French rapiers and poniards, with their assigns, as girdle, hangers, and so. And it would come to immediate trial, if your lordship would vouchsafe the answer.

Yes, why not? Let the foils be brought. If the gentleman is willing, and the king holds his purpose, I will win for him if I can. If not, I will gain nothing but my shame and the odd hits.

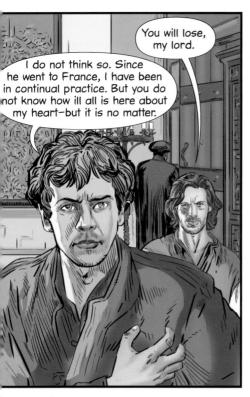

You will lose, my lord.

I do not think so. Since he went to France, I have been in continual practice. But you do not know how ill all is here about my heart—but it is no matter.

If your mind dislikes anything, obey it. I will forestall the match, saying you are not fit.

Not a whit, we defy augury. There is special providence in the fall of a sparrow. If it be now, it is not to come; if it be not to come, it will be now—the readiness is all.

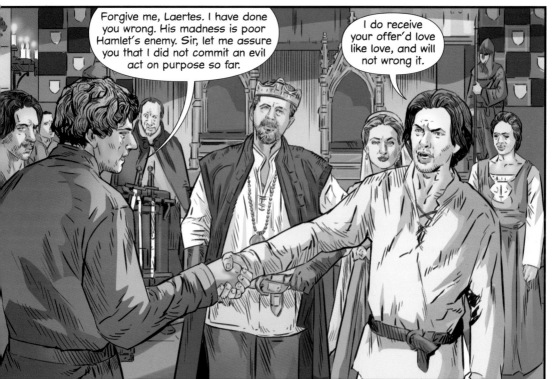

Forgive me, Laertes. I have done you wrong. His madness is poor Hamlet's enemy. Sir, let me assure you that I did not commit an evil act on purpose so far.

I do receive your offer'd love like love, and will not wrong it.

Give us the foils, come on. I will be your foil Laertes. Your skill shall shine against my ignorance like a star in the darkest night.

You mock me, sir.

Give them the foils, young Osric. Cousin Hamlet, you know the wager?

75

What happened, Laertes?

Why, I have fallen into my own trap, Osric. I am justly killed with mine own treachery.

What happened to the Queen?

She faints seeing you bleed.

No, no, the drink, the drink—O, my dear Hamlet—the drink—I am poisoned.

Oh villainy! Ho, let the door be locked! Treachery! Seek it out!

He is justly served. It is a poison temper'd by himself. Exchange forgiveness with me, noble Hamlet. Mine and my Father's death come not upon thee. Nor does your death come upon me.

Heaven make you free of it! I follow you.

I am dead, Horatio. Wretched Queen, adieu. You look pale, and tremble at this event, you are a quiet onlooker of this act. If I had time, I could tell you everything—but let it be. Horatio, you will live. Tell the world about me and my cause! Tell those who would want to know more!

Never believe that I shall live. There is some poisoned wine left in the cup.

No! Act like a man and give me the cup. Let go, for heaven's sake. O God, Horatio, if you ever did hold me in your heart, save my reputation in this harsh world when I am no more. Forget happiness for a while. Draw your breath in pain, and tell my true story!

What warlike noise is this?

That is young Fortinbras, fresh from his victory over Poland. Now he is challenging the ambassadors from England.

This quarry cries on havoc. O proud death, at feast is in progress your eternal cell that I have struck so many princes at a shot so bloodily?

This sight is dismal. And our news from England comes too late. The ears are senseless that should give us hearing to tell him his commandment is fulfilled. That Rosencrantz and Guildenstern are dead.

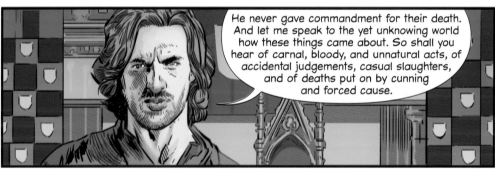

He never gave commandment for their death. And let me speak to the yet unknowing world how these things came about. So shall you hear of carnal, bloody, and unnatural acts, of accidental judgements, casual slaughters, and of deaths put on by cunning and forced cause.

Let us haste to hear it. With sorrow I embrace my fortune. I have some rights of memory in this kingdom, which invites me now to claim my rightful place here.

Of that I shall have also cause to speak. But let this same be presently performed, even while men's minds are wild, lest more mischance on plots and errors happen.

Let four captains bear Hamlet like a soldier to the stage. For he was likely, had he been put on, to have proved most royally: and for his passage, the soldiers' music and the rites of war speak loudly for him.

Go bid the soldiers shoot.

The End.

Glossary

For the curious ones...

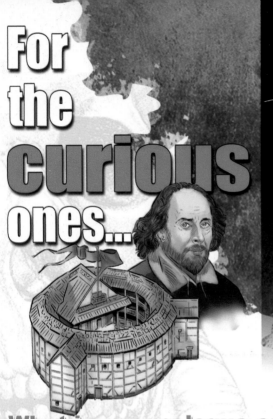

What is a tragedy?

William Shakespeare's *Hamlet* is known as a **'tragedy'**. The tragedy is a form of drama based on human suffering. It is known to invoke a sense of 'catharsis' or elation in the audience with the climax. The tradition of tragedy has a unique historical significance. It is strongly related to the cultural identity of the Western civilization. The form of tragedy originated in the theatre of ancient Greece 2,500 years ago. Since then, the tragedy has remained an important medium of cultural experimentation and change.

What is a monologue or a soliloquy?

A **'monologue'** is a long speech made by an actor in a play or a film. It is sometimes a solitary speech, used by a character to express his or her thoughts aloud. This is known as a **'soliloquy'**. However, sometimes a monologue is also directed at another character or the audience. The play *Hamlet* consists of many long monologues and soliloquies, some of which are quite famous. The "to be or not to be" soliloquy by Hamlet was even adopted as the plot device of a film called *To Be or Not To Be*.

The story behind Hamlet

Hamlet is one of the most well-known and poignant tragedies that William Shakespeare has written. Although there is dispute among scholars about the exact date of *Hamlet's* composition and performance, it is generally believed to have been composed around 1601. The play was performed at the wake of a religious upheaval – the Protestant Reformation movement.

There is also much debate on the text that influenced the play, but it is strongly believed that Shakespeare drew inspiration for Hamlet from the *Story of Amleth* written in the twelfth century, which first appeared in Saxo Grammaticus' *Historie Danicae* of 1514. The two stories have a lot in common. The Story of Amleth is about a prince who avenges his dead father by killing the murderer, his uncle, who is also the second husband of his mother. But the *Story of Amleth* does not end with the prince dying; instead, he becomes the next king. Shakespeare altered the ending to alleviate the play to the epic proportions of a tragedy.